A Commentary on the United Nations Convention
on the Rights of the Child

KW-482-689

Editors

André Alen, Johan Vande Lanotte, Eugeen Verhellen,
Fiona Ang, Eva Berghmans and Mieke Verheyde

Article 37

Prohibition of Torture, Death Penalty, Life Imprisonment and Deprivation of Liberty

By

William Schabas

Professor of Human Rights Law, National University of Ireland, Galway and
Director, Irish Centre for Human Rights

and

Helmut Sax

Ludwig Boltzmann Institute of Human Rights, Vienna

MARTINUS NIJHOFF PUBLISHERS
LEIDEN • BOSTON
2006

This book is printed on acid-free paper.

A Cataloging-in-Publication record for this book is available from the Library of Congress.

Cite as: W. Schabas and H. Sax, "Article 37. Prohibition of Torture, Death Penalty, Life Imprisonment and Deprivation of Liberty", in: A. Alen, J. Vande Lanotte, E. Verhellen, F. Ang, E. Berghmans and M. Verheyde (Eds.) *A Commentary on the United Nations Convention on the Rights of the Child* (Martinus Nijhoff Publishers, Leiden, 2006).

ISSN 1574-8626
ISBN 90-04-14886-8

© 2006 Koninklijke Brill NV, Leiden, The Netherlands.
Koninklijke Brill NV incorporates the imprints Brill Academic Publishers, Martinus Nijhoff Publishers and VSP.

Cover image by Nadia, 1 1/2 years old

http://www.brill.nl

PRINTED IN THE NETHERLANDS

CONTENTS

LIST OF ABBREVIATIONS

ACHPR	African Charter on Human and Peoples' Rights 1981
Beijing Rules	United Nations Standard Minimum Rules for the Administration of Juvenile Justice ('The Beijing Rules') 1985
CCPR	International Covenant on Civil and Political Rights 1966
CESCR Committee	UN Committee on Economic, Social and Cultural Rights
CRC	International Convention on the Rights of the Child 1989
CRC Committee	UN Committee on the Rights of the Child
ECHR	European Convention on Human Rights 1950
ECtHR	European Court of Human Rights
JDL Rules	United Nations Rules for the Protection of Juveniles Deprived of their Liberty 1990
Riyadh Guidelines	United Nations Guidelines for the Prevention of Juvenile Delinquency ('The Riyadh Guidelines') 1990
Tokyo Rules	United Nations Standard Minimum Rules for Non-custodial Measures ('The Tokyo Rules') 1990
UDHR	Universal Declaration of Human Rights 1948
UN	United Nations

AUTHOR BIOGRAPHY

William A. Schabas is director of the Irish Centre for Human Rights at the National University of Ireland, Galway, where he also holds the professorship in human rights law. In the past he was professor at the law school of the University of Quebec at Montreal, which he chaired for several years, and a member of the Quebec Human Rights Tribunal. Professor Schabas served as one of three international commissioners of the Sierra Leone Truth and Reconciliation Commission (2002–04). He is a national of Canada.

Professor Schabas holds post-graduate degrees in history and in law from universities in Canada. He is the author of twelve books and more than 150 articles dealing with such subjects as the abolition of capital punishment, international criminal prosecution and issues of transitional justice, in English and French. His writings have been translated into several languages, including Russian, German, Spanish, Portuguese, Chinese and Albanian. He has lectured around the world in the areas of international humanitarian and human rights law, and been a frequent participant in human rights fact-finding missions on behalf of international non-governmental organisations. He is an Officer in the Order of Canada.

Helmut Sax is based at the Ludwig Boltzmann Institute of Human Rights in Vienna, Austria. Following his legal studies at Vienna University he gained expertise in academic human rights legal research and training on a broad range of issues, including economic, social and cultural rights, development cooperation and structural aspects of domestic implementation of human rights standards. For several years now his work focuses on human rights of children, with emphasis on constitutional rights, child rights-based approaches, child refugees, trafficking and violence against children.

Mr. Sax has served as an expert member to the Austrian delegation to the UN GA Special Session on Children and he is also involved in its domestic follow-up, including both the preparation of the 2004 National Plan of Action for Children's Rights in Austria, when he co-chaired one of its preparatory working groups, and its current implementation process. Apart from academic writing, lectures and training he has worked as a child rights consultant, cooperating regularly with institutions, NGOs and National Coalitions.

ARTICLE 37

States Parties shall ensure that:

(a) No child shall be subjected to torture or other cruel, inhuman or degrading treatment or punishment. Neither capital punishment nor life imprisonment without possibility of release shall be imposed for offences committed by persons below eighteen years of age;

(b) No child shall be deprived of his or her liberty unlawfully or arbitrarily. The arrest, detention or imprisonment of a child shall be in conformity with the law and shall be used only as a measure of last resort and for the shortest appropriate period of time;

(c) Every child deprived of liberty shall be treated with humanity and respect for the inherent dignity of the human person and in a manner which takes into account the needs of persons of his or her age. In particular, every child deprived of liberty shall be separated from adults unless it is considered in the child's best interest not to do so and

ARTICLE 37

Les Etats parties veillent à ce que:

(a) Nul enfant ne soit soumis à la torture ni à des peines ou traitements cruels, inhumains ou dégradants. Ni la peine capitale ni l'emprisonnement à vie sans possibilité de libération ne doivent être prononcés pour les infractions commises par des personnes âgées de moins de dix-huit ans;

(b) Nul enfant ne soit privé de liberté de façon illégale ou arbitraire. L'arrestation, la détention ou l'emprisonnement d'un enfant doit être en conformité avec la loi, n'être qu'une mesure de dernier ressort, et être d'une durée aussi brève que possible;

(c) Tout enfant privé de liberté soit traité avec humanité et avec le respect dû à la dignité de la personne humaine, et d'une manière tenant compte des besoins des personnes de son âge. En particulier, tout enfant privé de liberté sera séparé des adultes, à moins que l'on estime préférable de ne pas le faire dans l'intérêt supérieur de l'enfant, et

shall have the right to maintain contact with his or her family through correspondence and visits, save in exceptional circumstances;

(d) Every child deprived of his or her liberty shall have the right to prompt access to legal and other appropriate assistance, as well as the right to challenge the legality of the deprivation of his or her liberty before a court or other competent, independent and impartial authority and to a prompt decision on any such action.

il a le droit de rester en contact avec sa famille par la correspondance et par les visites, sauf circonstances exceptionnelles;

(d) Les enfants privés de liberté aient le droit d'avoir rapidement accès à l'assistance juridique ou à toute autre assistance appropriée, ainsi que le droit de contester la légalité de leur privation de liberté devant un tribunal ou une autre autorité compétente, indépendante et impartiale, et à ce qu'une décision rapide soit prise en la matière.

PART I   PROHIBITION OF TORTURE, PROHIBITION OF DEATH PENALTY
AND LIFE IMPRISONMENT (ARTICLE 37(a))

William Schabas

CHAPTER ONE

INTRODUCTION*

1. Article 37 principally addresses issues relating to detention of the child. Although it is related to matters of criminal justice, because it speaks of torture and cruel, inhuman or degrading treatment, as well as arbitrary deprivation of liberty generally, it is also concerned with incarceration in psychiatric institutions and other manifestations of the deprivation of liberty.

Paragraph (a) of Article 37 is more specifically focussed on three distinct issues: torture and cruel, inhuman or degrading treatment, the death penalty and life imprisonment.

* March 2005. The author would like to thank Nicolas Rouleau for his assistance in researching the material in this article.

CHAPTER TWO

COMPARISON WITH RELATED INTERNATIONAL
HUMAN RIGHTS PROVISIONS

2. Article 37(a) expresses three principal norms with respect to the treatment of children. It prohibits torture and other cruel, inhuman or degrading treatment or punishment, capital punishment, and life imprisonment without the possibility of release.

3. The *prohibition of torture or other cruel, inhuman or degrading treatment* or punishment is a universal norm, applicable to adults as well as children. It is derived from texts that date back to the English Bill of Rights of 1688, which used the famous phrase 'cruel and unusual punishment'.[1] This concept was, of course, repeated in the eighth amendment to the United States Constitution of 1789, before making its appearance in one of the first international human rights instruments, the American Declaration of the Rights and Duties of Man. Article XXVI of that document, which predates the Universal Declaration of Human Rights (UDHR) by more than six months, prohibits 'cruel, infamous or unusual punishment' although it makes no reference to torture.[2]

The text of the first sentence of Article 37(a) finds its direct ancestor in Article 5 of the UDHR.[3] The same phrase has echoed through most of the subsequent human rights instruments, including Article 7 of the International Covenant on Civil and Political Rights (CCPR),[4] Article 5(2) of the American Convention on Human Rights,[5] Article 5 of the African Charter on Human and Peoples' Rights,[6] Article 17(2)(a) of the African Charter on the Rights and Welfare of the Child[7] and Article 13(c) of the Arab Charter on Human Rights.[8] The European Convention on Human Rights (ECHR) has its somewhat idiosyncratic text, referring to 'inhuman or degrading treatment or punishment' and omitting the word 'cruel' that appears in the Universal Declaration and all of the other texts.[9] The difference in wording would seem to be without

---

[1] 1 Wm. & Mary, 2d Sess., 1689, c. 2. See: A. F. Granucci, '"Nor cruel and unusual punishments inflicted": The original meaning', *California Law Review* 57, 1969, p. 839.
[2] OAS Doc. OAS/Ser.L/V/II.23, doc. 21, rev. 6.
[3] GA Res. 217A (III) (UN Doc A/810, 1948), at 71.
[4] (1976) 999 UNTS 171.
[5] OASTS No. 36, (1978) 1144 UNTS 123.
[6] OAU Doc. CAB/LEG/67/3 rev. 5.
[7] OAU Doc. CAB/LEG/24.9/49 (1990).
[8] Adopted by the League of Arab States, reprinted in *Human Rights Law Journal* 18, 1997, p. 151.
[9] (1955) 213 UNTS 221, ETC No. 5, Article 3.

significant legal consequences. There are also, of course, specialized conventions prohibiting torture and other cruel, inhuman or degrading treatment or punishment in the United Nations, European and Inter-American human rights systems.[10] A Trial Chamber of the International Criminal Tribunal for the former Yugoslavia has said that the prohibition on torture is a peremptory or *jus cogens* norm of customary international law: 'Because of the importance of the values it protects, this principle has evolved into a peremptory norm or *jus cogens*, that is, a norm that enjoys a higher rank in the international hierarchy than treaty law and even "ordinary" customary rules. The most conspicuous consequence of this higher rank is that the principle at issue cannot be derogated from by States through international treaties or local or special customs or even general customary rules not endowed with the same normative force.'[11]

4. The reference to imposition of *capital punishment* for crimes committed by persons under the age of eighteen reflects a similar norm that is set out in Article 6(5) of the CCPR. The prohibition on juvenile executions would seem to have been rather widely recognized in national justice systems for many years. It made its first appearance as an international norm in Article 68(4) of the fourth Geneva Convention of 1949.[12] However, in that instrument, it applies only to civilians in an occupied territory during international armed conflict. The authoritative Red Cross commentary on Article 68(4) states:

> 'The clause corresponds to similar provisions in the penal codes of many countries, and is based on the idea that a person who has not reached the age of eighteen years is not fully capable of sound judgment, does not always realize the significance of his actions and often acts under the influence of others, if not under constraint.'[13]

International humanitarian law later expanded the prohibition on juvenile executions to include a total ban on the death penalty for juveniles in 'offences related to the armed conflict'.[14]

The ECHR, adopted in 1950, imposes no such restriction on the death penalty in Article 2(1). It is not apparent that juvenile executions were ever carried out in

---

[10] Convention Against Torture and Other Cruel, Inhuman and Degrading Treatment or Punishment, GA Res. 39/46; European Convention for the Prevention of Torture and Inhuman or Degrading Treatment or Punishment, ETS. No. 126; Inter-American Convention to Prevent and Punish Torture, OASTS 67.

[11] ICTY, *Prosecutor v. Furundžija* (Case No. IT-95-17/1-T), Judgment, 10 December 1998, para. 153 (references omitted).

[12] *Geneva Convention of August 12, 1949 Relative to the Protection of Civilians* (1950) 75 UNTS 135.

[13] J. Pictet (ed.), *Commentary on the Geneva Convention relative to the Protection of Civilian Persons in Time of War* (ICRC, Geneva, 1956), pp. 346–347.

[14] *Protocol Additional I to the 1949 Geneva Conventions and Relating to The Protection of Victims of International Armed Conflicts*, (1979) 1125 UNTS 3, Article 77(5); *Protocol Additional II to the 1949 Geneva Conventions and Relating to The Protection of Victims of Non-International Armed Conflicts*, (1979) 1125 UNTS 609, 6(4).

States Parties to the European Convention before the death penalty became thoroughly abolished within Council of Europe Member States, in the mid-1990s.[15] The 1953 British Royal Commission on Capital Punishment reported that it was possible for sentence of death to be imposed on persons as young as twelve (India and Pakistan), fourteen (Canada) and sixteen (South Africa), but that the United Kingdom, France and Belgium all set an age limit of eighteen.[16] The European Union's Minimum Standards Paper on capital punishment issued in 1998, which is used by the European Union in its diplomatic initiatives with third States, declares: 'Capital punishment may not be imposed on: . . . persons below 18 years of age at the time of the commission of their crime.'[17]

The text of Article 6(5) of the CCPR reappears in Article 4(5) of the American Convention on Human Rights, but there is no reference whatsoever to the death penalty in the African Charter. The omission is corrected in Article 5(3) of the African Charter on the Rights and Welfare of the Child, which says that the '[d]eath sentence shall not be pronounced for crimes committed by children'. Similarly, the norm can be found in such 'soft law' instruments as the 'Safeguards Guaranteeing the Rights of those Facing the Death Penalty'[18] and the Standard Minimum Rules for the Administration of Juvenile Justice (the 'Beijing Rules').[19]

As for the Arab Charter, it prohibits imposing the death penalty on persons under the age of eighteen,[20] which is a somewhat different norm than what is expressed elsewhere. It is one thing to prohibit the death penalty for crimes committed while under the age of eighteen, and quite another to suggest that juvenile offenders will have to wait until they are eighteen so that they will be old enough to be executed!

The prohibition on executions for crimes committed under the age of eighteen is widely recognized as a norm of customary international law. In 2000, a resolution adopted by the United Nations Sub-Commission on the Protection and Promotion of Human Rights stated that 'international law concerning the imposition of the death penalty in relation to juveniles clearly establishes that the imposition of the death penalty on persons aged under 18 years at the time of the offence is in contravention of customary international law'.[21] In 2002, in a petition directed against

---

[15] See: H. G. Frank, *The Barbaric Punishment, Abolishing the Death Penalty* (The Hague/London/New York, Martinus Nijhoff Publishers, 2003).

[16] *Royal Commission on Capital Punishment 1949-1953, Report* (London, HMSO, 1953, Cmd. 8932), pp. 452–453.

[17] 'Guidelines for EU Policy Towards Third Countries on the Death Penalty', in: *European Union Annual Report on Human Rights, 11317/00*, p. 87. Note that Article 2(2) of the European Union Charter of Fundamental Rights OJ C 364/1, 18 December 2000, prohibits the death penalty under all circumstances.

[18] ESC Res. 1984/50 (UN Doc. E/1984/84, 1984), annex.

[19] UN Doc.A/Res. 40/33, 1985, annex, para. 17.2.

[20] OAU Doc. CAB/LEG/24.9/49 (1990), Article 12.

[21] UN Subcommission on the Promotion and the Protection of Human Rights, *The Death Penalty in Relation to Juvenile Offenders* (UN Doc. E/CN.4/Sub.2/RES/2000/17, 2000), para. 6.

the United States, the Inter-American Commission on Human Rights confirmed the customary nature of the prohibition on juvenile executions:

> [T]he Commission is satisfied, based upon the information before it, that this rule has been recognized as being of a sufficiently indelible nature to now constitute a norm of *jus cogens*, a development anticipated by the Commission in its Roach and Pinkerton decision. As noted above, nearly every nation state has rejected the imposition of capital punishment to individuals under the age of 18. They have done so through ratification of the ICCPR, U.N. Convention on the Rights of the Child, and the American Convention on Human Rights, treaties in which this proscription is recognized as nonderogable, as well as through corresponding amendments to their domestic laws. The acceptance of this norm crosses political and ideological boundaries and efforts to detract from this standard have been vigorously condemned by members of the international community as impermissible under contemporary human rights standards. Indeed, it may be said that the United States itself, rather than persistently objecting to the standard, has in several significant respects recognized the propriety of this norm by, for example, prescribing the age of 18 as the federal standard for the application of capital punishment and by ratifying the Fourth Geneva Convention without reservation to this standard. On this basis, the Commission considers that the United States is bound by a norm of *jus cogens* not to impose capital punishment on individuals who committed their crimes when they had not yet reached 18 years of age. As a *jus cogens* norm, this proscription binds the community of States, including the United States. The norm cannot be validly derogated from, whether by treaty or by the objection of a state, persistent or otherwise.[22]

5. The Convention on the Rights of the Child (hereafter CRC) is the only international instrument to prohibit *life imprisonment*, to the extent that there is no possibility of release, for crimes committed under the age of eighteen. There are, of course, general statements in a number of international human rights instruments and specialized documents dealing with criminal justice that argue against the possibility of life imprisonment without the possibility of release. For example, Article 10(3) of the CCPR states: 'The penitentiary system shall comprise treatment of prisoners the essential aim of which shall be their reformation and social rehabilitation.' Legislation preventing the eventual release of a prisoner who has demonstrated 'reformation and social rehabilitation' is arguably inconsistent with this provision.

---

[22] Inter-American Commission on Human Rights, *Domingues* v. *United States of America* (Case 12.285), Merits, Report N° 62/02, 22 October 2002, para. 85 (references omitted). The reference in the citation to the Roach and Pinkerton decision is to a ruling by the Commission in 1987 in which it said a prohibition on executions on persons for crimes committed under the age of eighteen was not yet a customary norm, but that such a norm was emerging. See: Inter-American Commission on Human Rights, *Roach & Pinkerton* v. *United States* (Case No. 9647), Resolution No. 3/87, reported in: OAS Doc. OEA/Ser.L/V/II.71 doc. 9 rev. 1, p. 147; *Inter-American Yearbook on Human Rights, 1987* (Dordrecht/Boston/London, Martinus Nijhoff, 1990), p. 328 and *Human Rights Law Journal* 8, p. 345.

CHAPTER THREE

SCOPE OF ARTICLE 37(A)

1. Drafting of Article 37(a)

6. The earliest version of Article 37(a) appears in the 1980 Working Party draft of the CRC. It contained a rather summary provision dealing with criminal procedure, which specified that a child shall not be liable to capital punishment, and that '[a]ny other punishment shall be adequate to the particular phase of his development'.[23] A more detailed provision had to wait until 1985, when Canada proposed a rather elaborate text guaranteeing the rights of a child upon being accused or convicted of a criminal offence.[24] The Canadian proposal included a statement that no child could be sentenced to death. It also added a new sentence: 'No child shall be subjected to cruel, inhuman or degrading treatment or punishment.' At the time, a 'child' was defined in the draft convention as being a person under eighteen, 'unless, under the law of his State, he has attained his age of majority earlier'.[25] The next year, Canada slightly revised its proposal, adding cross-references to the well-accepted provisions in international human rights law on which it was based: Article 5 of the UDHR, and Articles 6(5) and 7 of the CCPR. There was also a competing Polish text, but much to the same effect.[26]

7. In 1986, the draft provision was considerably reworked by the Commission on Human Rights. It is surely of significance that these discussions took place only a few months after the adoption, by the United Nations General Assembly, of the Standard Minimum Rules for the Administration of Juvenile Justice, known as the 'Beijing Rules'. They set out a relatively liberal and enlightened view of juvenile justice, and recognize the need for a fundamentally different approach to sentencing for criminal offences that are committed by juveniles. Paragraph 17(2) states that '[c]apital punishment shall not be imposed for any crime committed by juveniles'.[27] The Commentary to the Beijing Rules says this is 'in accordance with' Article 6(5) of the CCPR which, of course, it is not (the Covenant specifies eighteen years, whereas the Beijing Rules do not specify the age limit for 'juveniles'). The Beijing Rules also prohibit corporal punishment of children for criminal offences.[28]

---

[23] UN Doc. E/CN.4/1349, Article 20§2.
[24] UN Doc. E/CN.4/1985/64, Annex II, p. 4.
[25] UN Doc. E/CN.4/1985/64, Annex I, p. 2.
[26] UN Doc. A/C.3/40/3, para. 2.
[27] UN Doc.A/Res. 40/33, 1985.
[28] *Ibid.*, para. 17(3).

At the 1986 session of the Commission on Human Rights, an informal drafting party reworked the text, as follows: '. . . the States parties shall, in particular, ensure that: (a) No child is arbitrarily detained or subjected to torture, cruel, inhuman or degrading treatment or punishment; (b) Capital punishment or life imprisonment is not imposed for crimes committed by persons below eighteen years of age.'[29] By specifying the age, the text dispelled any uncertainty about the definition of the term 'child' in this context, and furthermore brought the provision into full compliance with Article 6(5) of the CCPR. But the new version also went beyond Article 6(5), including a prohibition on life imprisonment. This had not previously appeared in human rights treaty law. It also added the word 'torture', which Canada had inexplicably omitted, once again also making the text more consistent with the Covenant provision.

Paragraph (a) of the drafting party text, prohibiting torture and other cruel, inhuman or degrading treatment or punishment, was adopted by the Working Group without any change.[30] In fact, at no stage in the drafting of the Convention does this text ever appear to have elicited the slightest difficulty or controversy. Paragraph (b), dealing with the death penalty and life imprisonment, was another matter altogether. In the 1986 Working Group, the Japanese representative questioned the phrase 'or life imprisonment' and proposed its deletion.[31] According to the Working Group report, Canada sought to 'accommodate' the Japanese position and suggested adding the words 'without possibility of release' after the words 'life imprisonment'.[32]

The Report indicates that the United Kingdom also placed on record its objection to the provision, but does not suggest why.[33] Presumably, the United Kingdom was troubled by the life imprisonment reference, which was inconsistent with its legislation at the time.[34] In addition, the United States's representative objected to the draft paragraph, stating that reference to 'persons below eighteen years of age' was too arbitrary, and she proposed its deletion.[35] The official report of the discussions notes that Amnesty International and the International Commission of Jurists opposed the United States on this point.[36] The United States said that it did not consider the eighteen-year age limit to be 'an appropriate general rule', but added that it would not insist upon an amendment which would block consensus,

---

[29] UN Doc. E/CN.4/1986/39, para. 99.
[30] *Ibid.*, para. 103.
[31] *Ibid.*, para. 104.
[32] *Ibid.*
[33] *Ibid.*, para. 107.
[34] *E.g.*, ECtHR, *Hussain* v. *United Kingdom*, 21 February 1996, Series A, No 252; and ECtHR, *Singh* v. *United Kingdom*, 21 February 1996, Series A, No 280.
[35] UN Doc. E/CN.4/1986/39, paras. 105 and 107. The United States made such a statement concerning the draft provision on more than one occasion. See, for example: UN Doc. E/CN.4/1989/48, para. 544.
[36] *Ibid.*, para. 105.

providing it be understood that the United States maintained its right to make a reservation on this point.[37] Eventually, the Working Group adopted the following text: '. . . the States Parties to the present Convention shall, in particular, ensure that: (a) no child is arbitrarily detained or imprisoned or subjected to torture, cruel, inhuman or degrading treatment or punishment; (b) capital punishment or life imprisonment without possibility of release is not imposed for crimes committed by persons below 18 years of age'.[38]

8. The article was reviewed in a special Working Party session of the Commission on Human Rights in late 1988. Besides the Working Group text, the Working Party had another version proposed by the Crime, Prevention and Criminal Justice Branch of the Centre for Social Development and Humanitarian Affairs, United Nations Office at Vienna. The Vienna proposal revived the blanket prohibition on both capital punishment and life imprisonment, and indicated that this issue was still very much unresolved. The Crime Prevention Branch proposed the following: '. . . States parties shall ensure that: . . . (b) No child is subjected to torture, cruel, inhumane or degrading treatment, punishment or correction at any stage of justice administration; (c) The death penalty or a term of life imprisonment is not imposed for offences committed by children below 18 years of age'.[39] Venezuela also had prepared a proposal with a similar provision on torture, but nothing on the death penalty or life imprisonment.[40]

According to the report on the 1988 meeting, after a general debate, 'it became obvious that there was a total lack of consensus'.[41] The Chair appointed an open-ended drafting group that conceived the following proposal: 'No child shall be subjected to torture or other cruel, inhuman or degrading treatment or punishment. Neither capital punishment nor life imprisonment [without possibility of release] shall be imposed for offences committed by persons below 18 years of age.'[42] The square brackets indicated that the issue of life imprisonment without possibility of release had not been settled by consensus within the drafting group.

The report explains the proposed text of the drafting group: 'In introducing the proposal . . ., the representative of Portugal indicated that the drafting group had endeavoured to draw up a text consistent with the instruments adopted in this field by the United Nations, dividing the various independent situations which required protection into two articles. The new Article 19 therefore covered situations such as the prohibition of torture and other cruel, inhuman or degrading treatment or punishment, the death penalty or life imprisonment . . .'[43] This was

---

[37] *Ibid.*, paras. 105 and 107.
[38] UN Doc. E/CN.4/1988/WG.1/WP.1/Rev/.2. Article 19(2).
[39] UN Doc. E/CN.4/1988/WG.1/WP.2. Also: E/CN.4/1989/48, para. 534.
[40] UN Doc. E/CN.4/1988/WG.1/WP.11. Also: E/CN.4/1989/48, para. 535.
[41] UN Doc. E/CN.4/1989/48, para. 536. The proposal is found in: E/CN.4/1989/ WG.1/ WP.67/Rev.1.
[42] *Ibid.*
[43] *Ibid.*, para. 537.

only partially true. Although the prohibition of torture and of capital punishment for juveniles could hardly be contested as norms of existing human rights treaty law, the reference to life imprisonment was very much a matter of progressive development of the law, and no prior text existed on this subject.

First, there was a debate about form. Some delegations—East Germany, the Soviet Union and Italy—criticized the paragraph as lacking in homogeneity, because it combined 'manifest illegalities' such as torture with issues concerning punishment in accordance with due process of law.[44] Others—West Germany, Canada and Senegal—argued that the imposition of capital punishment on children was 'inhuman . . . treatment or punishment' and that therefore the paragraph was 'sufficiently homogeneous to be left as it stood'.[45] East Germany backed down on this point in the interests of consensus.

The Working Party then turned to the remaining point in dispute, namely the suggestion that life imprisonment would be acceptable to the extent there was the possibility of release. Austria, West Germany, Senegal and Venezuela all argued for deletion of 'without possibility of release'. China, India, Japan, Norway, the Soviet Union and the United States of America argued for its retention. India and Norway explained that they could not join a consensus to delete the words on what were essential technical grounds: this would profoundly change a text adopted at the first reading of the provision that they had supported.[46]

China, the Federal Republic of Germany, the Netherlands and Venezuela suggested removing all reference to life imprisonment, in order to promote a consensus.[47] Senegal stubbornly insisted it be retained. But the only way to agree upon a text that referred to life imprisonment was to include the troublesome phrase 'without possibility of release', and this is indeed what happened.[48] The Working Party draft[49] was adopted by the Commission on Human Rights by consensus,[50] by the Third Committee in an unrecorded vote,[51] and ultimately by the General Assembly.[52]

2. Reservations to Article 37(a)

9. Reservations are specifically permitted by Article 51 of the CRC, providing they are not contrary to the 'object and purpose' of the treaty. Although there is no

---

[44] *Ibid.*, para. 540.
[45] *Ibid.*
[46] *Ibid.*, para. 541.
[47] *Ibid.*, para. 542.
[48] *Ibid.*, paras. 542–543.
[49] UN Doc. E/CN.4/1989/48/Rev.1, p. 15.
[50] UN Doc. E/CN.4/1989/L.88. The debates are found at UN Doc. E/CN.4/1989/SR.54, UN Doc. E/CN.4/1989/SR.55, UN Doc. E/CN.4/1989/SR.55/Add.1.
[51] UN Doc. A/C.3/SR.44, para. 63, UN Doc. A/C.3/44/L.44.
[52] UN Doc. A/44/PV.61, as GA Res. 44/25.

express reference in the CRC, it is reasonable to presume the application of the regime dealing with reservations set out in Articles 19 to 23 of the Vienna Convention on the Law of Treaties, which in any case is widely considered to constitute a codification of customary norms. Article 51 of the CRC establishes the same 'object and purpose' test for the legality of reservations as the Vienna Convention, but it does not spell out the procedural issues, such as the submission of objections, something addressed in the Vienna Convention.

10. Three States have formulated reservations to Article 37 of the Convention. They are all neighbours: Myanmar, Singapore and Malaysia. The three reservations are targeted at Article 37 generally, and there is nothing in their text to suggest any particular relevance with respect to the issues contemplated by Article 37(a). None of these States is alleged to practice juvenile executions.

Myanmar's reservation to Article 37, formulated at the time of accession on 15 July 1991, was withdrawn on 19 October 1993, but not before Germany and Portugal had objected that the reservation was incompatible with the object and purpose of the Convention. Ireland also objected to the Myanmar reservation, but well beyond the twelve-month deadline imposed by Article 20(5) of the Vienna Convention on the Law of Treaties and, moreover, some two years after the withdrawal of the reservation by Myanmar.

Malaysia and Singapore both acceded to the Convention in 1995, and their reservations inspired a wave of objections from European States. Germany, Finland, Austria, the Netherlands, Sweden, Norway, Belgium, Denmark and Ireland[53] have all objected to the Malaysian reservation. Germany, Belgium, Italy, the Netherlands, Finland, Norway, Portugal and Sweden have formulated objections to the reservation by Singapore.

11. At the time the CRC was being drafted, on at least two occasions the United States of America reserved its right to make reservations to Article 37(a) of the Convention. However, no such reservation was actually submitted at the time of its signature, on 16 February 1995. In contrast, the United States formulated a very controversial reservation to Article 6(5) of the CCPR at the time of ratification. The failure of the United States to formulate a reservation at the time of signature contributes to the argument that it was not a 'persistent objector' to the emergence of a customary legal norm prohibiting juvenile executions or, for that matter, life imprisonment of young offenders without the possibility of parole.

---

[53] Once again, Ireland's objection was submitted well past the twelve-month deadline.

3. Content of the Norm

3.1   Torture and Other Cruel, Inhuman or Degrading
Treatment or Punishment

12. The prohibition of torture and other cruel, inhuman or degrading treatment or punishment is at the core of modern human rights law. The norm has been exhaustively interpreted in the case law of the European Commission and Court of Human Rights,[54] and the United Nations Human Rights Committee and Committee Against Torture, not to mention the jurisprudence of national constitutional courts.

The distinction between the two broad categories is said to be one of degree. The 1975 General Assembly resolution on torture said '[t]orture constitutes an aggravated form of cruel, inhuman or degrading treatment or punishment'.[55] According to the European Court of Human Rights, torture is addressed distinctly in order to attach a 'special stigma to deliberate inhuman treatment causing very serious and cruel suffering'.[56]

With hindsight, it is intriguing to consider the ultimate legal effect of this provision of the CRC had it been left to stand alone, without any reference to either the death penalty or to life imprisonment in the second sentence of Article 37(a). There is now considerable authority for the proposition that both of these forms of extreme punishment are prohibited by the norm against 'torture and other forms of cruel, inhuman or degrading treatment or punishment'. In addition to relevant decisions by various national constitutional courts,[57] support can be found in Article 77 of the Rome Statute of the International Criminal Court, which sets life imprisonment subject to a mandatory review after twenty-five years as the maximum penalty for genocide, war crimes and crimes against humanity.[58] The reference to life imprisonment in the CRC has the unfortunate consequence of restricting the evolution of the general prohibition on torture and cruel, inhuman or degrading treatment or punishment, in much the same way as Article 3 of the ECHR has been restricted in scope by the reference to capital punishment in Article 2(1) of the Convention.[59]

---

[54] See, *e.g.*, R. Morgan and M. Evans, *Combating Torture in Europe* (Strasbourg, Council of Europe Publishing, 2001).

[55] 'Declaration on the protection of all persons from being subjected to torture and other cruel, inhuman or degrading treatment or punishment', (GA Res. 3452), 1975), Article 1.

[56] ECtHR, *Ireland v. United Kingdom*, 18 January 1978, Series A, No 25, para. 167.

[57] See, for example: *S. v. Makwanyane*, [1995] (3) SA 391; *United States v. Burns*, [2001] 1 SCR 183. The German Constitutional Court has said that life imprisonment without possibility of parole constitutes cruel, inhuman or degrading punishment: [1977] 45 BVerfGE 187, 228. See generally: D. van Zyl Smit, 'Is Life Imprisonment Constitutional?—The German Experience', *Public Law* 263, 1992.

[58] Rome Statute of the International Criminal Court (UN Doc. A/CONF.183/9,1998), as corrected by the *procès-verbaux* of November 10, 1998, and July 12, 1999. See: W. A. Schabas, *Introduction to the International Criminal Court*, 2nd ed. (Cambridge, Cambridge University Press, 2004).

[59] ECtHR, *Soering v. United Kingdom and Germany*, 7 July 1989, Series A, No 161, 11 EHRR 439 and ECtHR, *Öcalan v. Turkey*, 12 March 2003, *Reports* 2003, paras. 188–199.

The principal discussions on adoption of what would become Article 37(a) took place within a few months of the adoption of the Beijing Rules. In addition to a prohibition on capital punishment for juveniles, the Beijing Rules also prohibit corporal punishment of children for criminal offences.[60] This may help to explain why the reference to torture and other cruel, inhuman or degrading treatment or punishment was added at the time.[61] The Beijing Rules say nothing on the subject of life imprisonment.

3.1.1   Torture

13. The definition of torture in Article 1(1) of the United Nations Convention Against Torture and Other Cruel, Inhuman or Degrading Treatment or Punishment is widely accepted: 'torture means any act by which severe pain or suffering, whether physical or mental, is intentionally inflicted on a person for such purposes as obtaining from him or a third person information or a confession, punishing him for an act he or a third person has committed or is suspected of having committed, or intimidating or coercing him or a third person, or for any reason based on discrimination of any kind, when such pain or suffering is inflicted by or at the instigation of or with the consent or acquiescence of a public official or other person acting in an official capacity. It does not include pain or suffering arising only from, inherent in or incidental to lawful sanctions.' Rulings of the *ad hoc* international criminal tribunals have taken a somewhat different approach. After initially endorsing the definition in Article 1 of the Torture Convention,[62] they subsequently rejected its wholesale application because of the 'public official' requirement. According to a Trial Chamber in *Prosecutor* v. *Kvočka*, 'the state actor requirement imposed by international human rights law is inconsistent with the application of individual criminal responsibility for international crimes found in international humanitarian law and international criminal law'.[63] However, this reasoning does not apply with respect to the CRC, for which the definition in Article 1 of the Torture Convention should be retained.

14. Although it does not do so cavalierly, the CRC Committee (hereafter: CRC Committee) has made several charges of torture for which it holds States Parties

---

[60] UN Doc.A/Res. 40/33, 1985, annex, paras. 17(2) and 17(3).

[61] The European Court of Human Rights had earlier found corporal punishment to be prohibited by article 3 of the ECHR, which is essentially comparable to article 7 of the International Covenant.

[62] ICTY, *Prosecutor v. Delalić* et al. (Case No. IT-96-21), Judgment, 16 November 1998, para. 494–496. Also: ICTY, *Prosecutor v. Furundžija* (Case No. IT-95-17/1-T), Judgment, 10 December 1998, para. 159; ICTY, *Prosecutor v. Furundžija* (Case No. Case No. IT-95-17/1-A), Judgment, 21 July 2000, para. 111; ICTR, *Prosecutor v. Akayesu* (Case No. ICTR-96-4-T), Judgment, 2 September 1998, paras. 593–595, 681.

[63] ICTY, *Prosecutor v. Kunarac* (Case No. IT-96-23 & IT-96-23/1-A), Judgment, 12 June 2002, paras. 146–148.

to be responsible. Those who have been criticized recently include Romania,[64] Kazakhstan,[65] Ukraine,[66] India,[67] Uzbekistan,[68] Cameroon,[69] Guatemala,[70] Democratic Republic of the Congo,[71] Turkey,[72] Tajikistan,[73] Kyrgyzstan,[74] Colombia,[75] Israel[76] and Tunisia.[77] In some cases, specific reference has been made to the use of torture for the purpose of extracting confessions.[78]

15. Generally, States Parties themselves do not provide admissions of torture within the materials they submit to the CRC Committee. In fact, some States, such as Romania[79] and Israel,[80] have gone to great lengths in their reports to emphasize the provisions for the prevention of torture in their domestic legislation and in the conventions to which they are parties. Presumably the Committee relies upon various NGO sources, but in this respect it has also made specific reference on occasion to the reports of the Special Rapporteur on Torture of the Commission on Human Rights,[81] and to the concluding observations of the Committee Against

---

[64] CRC Committee, *Concluding Observations: Romania* (UN Doc. CRC/C/15/Add.199, 2003), para. 34.

[65] CRC Committee, *Concluding Observations: Kazakhstan* (UN Doc. CRC/C/15/Add.213, 2003), para. 36.

[66] CRC Committee, *Concluding Observations:* Ukraine (UN Doc. CRC/C/15/Add.191, 2002), para. 35.

[67] CRC Committee, *Concluding Observations: India* (UN Doc. CRC/C/15/Add.228, 2004), para. 42.

[68] CRC Committee, *Concluding Observations: Uzbekistan* (UN Doc. CRC/C/15/Add.167, 2001), para. 39.

[69] CRC Committee, *Concluding Observations: Cameroon* (UN Doc. CRC/C/15/Add.164, 2001), para. 34.

[70] CRC Committee, *Concluding Observations: Guatemala* (UN Doc. CRC/C/15/Add.154, 2001), para. 54.

[71] CRC Committee, *Concluding Observations: Democratic Republic of the Congo',* (UN Doc. CRC/C/15/Add.153, 2001), para. 32.

[72] CRC Committee, *Concluding Observations: Turkey* (UN Doc. CRC/C/15/Add.152, 2001), para. 39.

[73] CRC Committee, *Concluding Observations: Tajikistan,* (UN Doc. CRC/C/15/Add.136), para. 28.

[74] CRC Committee, *Concluding Observations: Kyrgyzstan* (UN Doc. CRC/C/15/Add.127, 2000), para. 33.

[75] CRC Committee, *Concluding Observations: Colombia* (UN Doc. CRC/C/15/Add.137, 2000), para. 34.

[76] CRC Committee, *Concluding Observations: Israel* (UN Doc. CRC/C/15/Add.195, 2002), para. 36.

[77] CRC Committee, *Concluding Observations: Tunisia* (UN Doc. CRC/C/15/Add.181, 2002), para. 31.

[78] CRC Committee, *Concluding Observations: Kazakhstan* (UN Doc. CRC/C/15/Add.213, 2003), para. 36.

[79] CRC Committee, *Second periodic report of Romania* (UN Doc. CRC/C/65/Add.19, 2002), paras. 168–171.

[80] CRC Committee, *Periodic report of Israel* (UN Doc. CRC/C/8/Add.44, 2002), paras. 400–402.

[81] CRC Committee, *Concluding Observations: Romania* (UN Doc. CRC/C/15/Add.199, 2003), para. 34; *Cameroon* (UN Doc. CRC/C/15/Add.164, 2001), para. 34.

Torture and the Human Rights Committee.[82] The CRC Committee has expressed its concern that El Salvador was not able to provide information or give an estimate of the number of registered cases of torture in its internment centres for juvenile offenders.[83] Similarly, it remarked on the lack of information from Myanmar, 'especially in the light of numerous reports received of torture'.[84] In the few cases where States recognize the presence of torture, they blame it on extrinsic factors such as war, kidnapping or poverty, and emphasize their own good faith efforts to prosecute the individuals responsible.[85]

16. The CRC Committee has been critical of States for non-existence or inadequate codification of the prohibition of torture in their domestic criminal law.[86] Occasionally the comments have seemed a bit gratuitous, for example, when the Committee criticized Costa Rica for having no explicit legislation prohibiting the use of torture, after acknowledging 'that no cases of torture of children have been reported in the State party'.[87] Actually, all that the Convention Against Torture requires is that all 'acts of torture' be punishable, and most countries effect this with their ordinary criminal law prohibitions of assault. As a general rule, criminal law systems do not require special legislation in order to deal with torture, as the Human Rights Committee noted in its General Comment No. 7.[88] In fact, incorporating the definition, with its special elements, merely complicates the task of prosecutors in dealing with the issue. The flip side of the problem can be seen in the Dominican Republic, where the CRC Committee noted a 'clear legislative prohibition', but one accompanied by persistent reports of conduct to the contrary.[89]

Although Rwanda has enacted legislation prohibiting torture and cruel, inhuman or degrading treatment or punishment against children, the CRC Committee criticized Rwanda for failing to define torture in the legislation.[90] This is a curious observation, because definitions usually serve to narrow the scope of general terms, and one might well conclude that the absence of a definition in Rwandan law assists

---

[82] CRC Committee, *Concluding Observations: Cameroon* (UN Doc. CRC/C/15/Add.164, 2001), para. 34.

[83] CRC Committee, *Concluding Observations: El Salvador* (UN Doc. CRC/C/15/Add.232, 2004), para. 35.

[84] CRC Committee, *Report on the thirty-sixth session*, (UN Doc. CRC/C/140, 2004), para. 414.

[85] CRC Committee, *Second periodic report of Guatemala* (UN Doc. CRC/C/65/Add.10, 2000), paras. 122–126.

[86] CRC Committee, *Concluding Observations: Ukraine* (UN Doc. CRC/C/15/Add.191, 2002), para. 35.

[87] CRC Committee, *Concluding Observations: Costa Rica* (UN Doc. CRC/C/15/Add.117, 2000), para. 18.

[88] Human Rights Committee, *General Comment No. 7: Torture or cruel, inhuman or degrading treatment or punishment (Art.7)*, 1982, para. 1.

[89] CRC Committee, *Concluding Observations: Dominican Republic* (UN Doc. CRC/C/15/Add.150, 2001), para. 28.

[90] CRC Committee, *Report on the thirty-sixth session* (UN Doc. CRC/C/140, 2004), para. 195.

prosecution of the offence of torture. The CRC Committee has criticized Ukraine because its Criminal Code fails to declare evidence extracted under torture to be inadmissible,[91] something that is a requirement under Article 15 of the Convention Against Torture. The CRC Committee has also criticized States Parties for their failure to investigate and prosecute alleged perpetrators of torture.[92]

3.1.2   *Cruel, Inhuman or Degrading Treatment or Punishment*

17. 'Cruel, inhuman or degrading treatment or punishment' is not defined in the Convention Against Torture, which treats it as a residual category for acts that do not rise to the level of torture.[93] The Human Rights Committee has said that '[i]t may not be necessary to draw sharp distinctions between the various prohibited forms of treatment or punishment. These distinctions depend on the kind, purpose and severity of the particular treatment.'[94]

18. The CRC Committee has identified several specific manifestations of cruel, inhuman or degrading treatment or punishment within States Parties, and commented on these in its concluding observations. These include violations concerning conditions of detention, including psychological intimidation, holding children in solitary confinement and police brutality. The Committee has also referred to rape and sexual violence against children as manifestations of cruel, inhuman or degrading treatment. Several countries have been criticized for the practice of corporal punishment. The Committee has also, but not systematically, referred in a generic sense to acts of cruel, inhuman or degrading treatment or punishment. Several States have been cited in recent reports as being responsible for violations of the norm, including Tunisia,[95] Cameroon,[96] Madagascar,[97] Côte d'Ivoire,[98] Democratic Republic of the Congo,[99] and the Dominican Republic.[100]

---

[91] CRC Committee, *Concluding Observations: Ukraine* (UN Doc. CRC/C/15/Add.191, 2002), paras. 35–36.

[92] CRC Committee, *Concluding Observations: Uzbekistan* (UN Doc. CRC/C/15/Add.167, 2001), para. 39; '*Turkey* (UN Doc. CRC/C/15/Add.152, 2001), para. 39.

[93] GA Res. 39/46, annex, Article 16(1).

[94] Human Rights Committee, *General Comment No. 7: Torture or cruel, inhuman or degrading treatment or punishment (Art.7)*, para. 2.

[95] CRC Committee, *Concluding Observations: Tunisia* (UN Doc. CRC/C/15/Add.181, 2002), para. 31.

[96] CRC Committee, *Concluding Observations: Cameroon* (UN Doc. CRC/C/15/Add.164, 2001), para. 34.

[97] CRC Committee, *Concluding Observations: Madagascar* (UN Doc. CRC/C/15/Add.218, 2003), para. 38.

[98] CRC Committee, *Concluding Observations: Côte d'Ivoire* (UN Doc. CRC/C/15/Add.155, 2001), para. 30.

[99] CRC Committee, *Concluding Observations: Democratic Republic of the Congo* (UN Doc. CRC/C/15/Add.153, 2001), para. 32.

[100] CRC Committee, *Concluding Observations Dominican Republic* (UN Doc. CRC/C/15/Add.150, 2001), para. 28.

19. Somewhat more frequently, the Committee uses the term 'ill-treatment'. It is not evident whether 'ill-treatment' is simply shorthand for 'cruel, inhuman or degrading treatment or punishment', or rather whether it is a euphemism adopted by the Committee in order to make the bitter pill of criticism for violation of Article 37(a) slightly easier to swallow. Concluding observations have noted reports of 'ill-treatment' in India,[101] Uzbekistan,[102] Kenya,[103] Guatemala,[104] Democratic Republic of the Congo,[105] Tajikistan,[106] Turkey,[107] Kyrgyzstan,[108] Dominican Republic,[109] Italy,[110] Mauritania,[111] Israel,[112] El Salvador,[113] Myanmar,[114] Romania,[115] Madagascar,[116] Cyprus,[117] Zambia,[118] Morocco,[119] Ukraine,[120] and Haiti.[121] Often the references to 'ill-treatment' refer specifically to acts perpetrated by the police or members of the security forces.

---

[101] CRC Committee, *Concluding Observations: India* (UN Doc. CRC/C/15/Add.228, 2004), para. 42.
[102] CRC Committee, *Concluding Observations: Uzbekistan* (UN Doc. CRC/C/15/Add.167, 2001), para. 39.
[103] CRC Committee, *Concluding Observations: Kenya* (UN Doc. CRC/C/15/Add.160, 2001), para. 35.
[104] CRC Committee, *Concluding Observations: Guatemala* (UN Doc. CRC/C/15/Add.154, 2001), para. 54.
[105] CRC Committee, *Concluding Observations: Democratic Republic of the Congo* (UN Doc. CRC/C/15/Add.153, 2001), para. 74.
[106] CRC Committee, *Concluding Observations: Tajikistan* (UN Doc. CRC/C/15/Add.136, 2000), para. 28.
[107] CRC Committee, *Concluding Observations: Turkey* (UN Doc. CRC/C/15/Add.152, 2001), para. 39.
[108] CRC Committee, *Concluding Observations: Kyrgyzstan* (UN Doc. CRC/C/15/Add.127, 2000), para. 33.
[109] CRC Committee, *Concluding Observations: Dominican Republic* (UN Doc. CRC/C/15/Add.150, 2001), para. 28.
[110] CRC Committee, *Concluding Observations: Italy* (UN Doc. CRC/C/15/Add.198, 2003), para. 31.
[111] CRC Committee, *Concluding Observations: Mauritania* (UN Doc. CRC/C/15/Add.159, 2001), para. 51.
[112] CRC Committee, *Concluding Observations: Israel* (UN Doc. CRC/C/15/Add.195, 2002), para. 36.
[113] CRC Committee, *Concluding Observations: El Salvador* (UN Doc. CRC/C/15/Add.232, 2004), para. 35.
[114] CRC Committee, *Report on the thirty-sixth session* (UN Doc. CRC/C/140, 2004), para. 414.
[115] CRC Committee, *Concluding Observations: Romania* (UN Doc. CRC/C/15/Add.199, 2003), para. 34.
[116] CRC Committee, *Concluding Observations: Madagascar* (UN Doc. CRC/C/15/Add.218, 2003), para. 289.
[117] CRC Committee, *Concluding Observations: Cyprus* (UN Doc. CRC/C/15/Add.205, 2003), para. 34.
[118] CRC Committee, *Concluding Observations: Zambia* (UN Doc. CRC/C/15/Add.206, 2003), para. 32.
[119] CRC Committee, *Concluding Observations: Morocco* (UN Doc. CRC/C/15/Add.211, 2003), para. 34.
[120] CRC Committee, *Concluding Observations: Ukraine* (UN Doc. CRC/C/15/Add.191, 2002), para. 36.
[121] CRC Committee, *Concluding Observations: Haiti* (UN Doc. CRC/C/15/Add.202, 2003), para. 62.

Harsh conditions of detention are often cited by the Committee as amounting to cruel, inhuman or degrading treatment prohibited by Article 37(a). This has been reported in recent concluding observations concerning Guyana,[122] Burkina Faso,[123] Madagascar,[124] Syria[125] and Haiti.[126] The Committee has even criticized States for 'the high number of children in [their] prisons who are detained in poor conditions, often together with adult offenders' on the basis that it *might* render children 'vulnerable to abuse and ill-treatment'.[127] There have been specific reports of 'psychological intimidation' of detained children concerning Uzbekistan,[128] Tajikistan,[129] and Kyrgyzstan,[130] although it is hard to believe that this is merely a regional phenomenon. Often, the practices are simply referred to in a general and somewhat colloquial sense as 'police brutality': Tanzania,[131] Argentina,[132] Suriname,[133] South Africa,[134] Mali.[135]

20. In one of its General Comments on torture, the Human Rights Committee said that '[e]ven such a measure as solitary confinement may, according to the circumstances, and especially when the person is kept incommunicado, be contrary' to the prohibition.[136] In its second General Comment on torture, the Human Rights Committee referred somewhat more cautiously to 'prolonged solitary confinement'.[137] In its comments on Singapore, the CRC Committee expressed concern that

---

[122] CRC Committee, *Concluding Observations: Guyana* (UN Doc. CRC/C/15/Add.224, 2004), para. 55.
[123] CRC Committee, *Concluding Observations: Burkina Faso* (UN Doc. CRC/C/15/Add.193, 2002), para. 30.
[124] CRC Committee, *Concluding Observations: Madagascar* (UN Doc. CRC/C/15/Add.218, 2003), para. 38.
[125] CRC Committee, *Concluding Observations: Syria* (UN Doc. CRC/C/15/Add.212, 2003), para. 52.
[126] CRC Committee, *Concluding Observations: Haiti* (UN Doc. CRC/C/15/Add.202, 2003), para. 62.
[127] CRC Committee, *Concluding Observations: Pakistan* (UN Doc. CRC/C/15/Add.217, 2003), para. 80.
[128] CRC Committee, *Concluding Observations: Uzbekistan* (UN Doc. CRC/C/15/Add.167, 2001), para. 39.
[129] CRC Committee, *Concluding Observations: Tajikistan* (UN Doc. CRC/C/15/Add.136, 2000), para. 28.
[130] CRC Committee, *Concluding Observations: Kyrgyzstan* (UN Doc. CRC/C/15/Add.127, 2000), para. 33.
[131] CRC Committee, *Concluding Observations: Tanzania* (UN Doc. CRC/C/15/Add.156, 2001), para. 36.
[132] CRC Committee, *Concluding Observations: Argentina* (UN Doc. CRC/C/15/Add.187, 2002), para. 36.
[133] CRC Committee, *Concluding Observations: Suriname* (UN Doc. CRC/C/15/Add.130, 2000), para. 33.
[134] CRC Committee, *Concluding Observations: South Africa* (UN Doc. CRC/C/15/Add.122, 2000), para. 21.
[135] CRC Committee, *Concluding Observations: Mali* (UN Doc. CRC/C/15/Add.113, 1999), para. 21.
[136] Human Rights Committee, *General Comment No. 7: Torture or cruel, inhuman or degrading treatment or punishment (Art.7)*, para. 2.
[137] Human Rights Committee, *General Comment No. 20: Replaces general comment 7 concerning prohibition of torture and cruel treatment or punishment (Art. 7)*, 1992, para. 6.

solitary confinement was used 'to discipline juvenile offenders'.[138] The concluding observations on the United Kingdom refer to the placement of juvenile detainees in solitary confinement in prisons.[139] In Turkey, the CRC Committee noted the police or *genderma* practice of holding children incommunicado and denying them access to legal counsel.[140]

21. Sometimes cruel, inhuman or degrading treatment or punishment takes on a dimension of ethnic persecution. In this context, it is worth recalling Article 2(1) of the CRC, which imposes on all States Parties the obligation to 'ensure the rights set forth in the present Convention to each child within their jurisdiction without discrimination of any kind, irrespective of the child's or his or her parent's or legal guardian's race, colour, sex, language, religion, political or other opinion, national, ethnic or social origin, property, disability, birth or other status'. In its comments on Israel, the CRC Committee noted that the victims of ill-treatment were generally Palestinian children.[141] In its concluding observations on Slovakia, the Committee said it was 'concerned at the persistence of acts of violence by groups, particularly skinheads, directed towards Roma and their children and other ethnic minorities, and at continuous allegations that the police and prosecutors have failed to investigate acts of racially motivated violence promptly and effectively, and have been reluctant to identify a racial motive behind such attacks'.[142] Reports of ill-treatment and even torture of Roma children have been reported with respect to Ukraine.[143] Italy has been cited for 'the prevalence of abuse' by law enforcement officers 'in particular against foreign and Roma children'.[144] Similarly, the Committee has expressed concern about allegations against Swiss law enforcement officers of ill-treatment of 'foreign children'.[145]

22. The case law of the *ad hoc* international criminal tribunals has greatly developed the significance of rape and other forms of sexual violence as breaches of the norm prohibiting torture and other cruel, inhuman or degrading treatment or punishment. Thus, the Appeals Chamber of the International Criminal Tribunal for

---

[138] CRC Committee, *Concluding Observations: Singapore* (UN Doc. CRC/C/15/Add.220, 2003), para. 44.

[139] CRC Committee, *Concluding Observations: United Kingdom* (UN Doc. CRC/C/15/Add.188, 2002), para. 33.

[140] CRC Committee, *Concluding Observations: Turkey* (UN Doc. CRC/C/15/Add.152, 2001), para. 39.

[141] CRC Committee, *Concluding Observations: Israel* (UN Doc. CRC/C/15/Add.195, 2002), para. 36.

[142] CRC Committee, *Concluding Observations: Slovakia* (UN Doc. CRC/C/15/Add.140, 2000), para. 25.

[143] CRC Committee, *Concluding Observations: Ukraine* (UN Doc. CRC/C/15/Add.191, 2002), para. 36.

[144] CRC Committee, *Concluding Observations: Italy* (UN Doc. CRC/C/15/Add.198, 2003), para. 31.

[145] CRC Committee, *Concluding Observations: Switzerland* (UN Doc. CRC/C/15/Add.182, 2002), para. 30.

the former Yugoslavia has said that '[s]exual violence necessarily gives rise to severe pain or suffering, whether physical or mental, and in this way justifies its characterisation as an act of torture. Severe pain or suffering, as required by the definition of the crime of torture, can thus be said to be established once rape has been proved, since the act of rape necessarily implies such pain or suffering.'[146] The CRC Committee has not made the equation between torture and rape or sexual abuse, but it has on occasion referred to such matters more generally in the context of Article 37(a). In concluding observations on India, for example, the Committee stated its concern 'at numerous reports' of 'sexual abuse of children in detention facilities'.[147] With respect to Myanmar, the Committee cited 'numerous reports received' concerning 'rape of children by law enforcement officials and army personnel'.[148] The concluding observations on Sudan spoke of 'acts of torture, rape and other cruel, inhuman or degrading treatment ... committed against children in the context of the armed conflict'.[149]

23. The CRC makes no reference to the phenomenon of 'forced disappearance', perhaps because it had not yet fully attracted the attention of international human rights bodies when the instrument was being drafted. Occasionally, the CRC Committee has commented on the phenomenon within the context of Article 37(a). Forced disappearance is mentioned with respect to Cameroon[150] and Colombia.[151] Likewise, the Committee has also cited cases of extrajudicial killing or execution: India,[152] Cameroon,[153] Colombia.[154] Concluding observations on Argentina spoke of the phenomenon of 'easy trigger syndrome' (*gatillo fácil*) among law enforcement officials.[155] The Committee referred to such executions for the purpose of 'social cleansing' of street children in its remarks on Guatemala.[156] Both of these areas, forced disappearance and extrajudicial execution, are in many ways more properly

---

[146] ICTY, *Prosecutor* v. *Kunarac, o.c.*(note 63), para. 149–151.

[147] CRC Committee, *Concluding Observations: India* (UN Doc. CRC/C/15/Add.228, 2004), para. 42.

[148] CRC Committee, *Report on the thirty-sixth session* (UN Doc. CRC/C/140, 2004), para. 414.

[149] CRC Committee, *Concluding Observations: Sudan* (UN Doc. CRC/C/15/Add.190, 2002), para. 35.

[150] CRC Committee, *Concluding Observations: Cameroon* (UN Doc. CRC/C/15/Add.164, 2001), para. 34.

[151] CRC Committee, *Concluding Observations: Colombia* (UN Doc. CRC/C/15/Add.137, 2000), para. 34.

[152] CRC Committee, *Concluding Observations: India* (UN Doc. CRC/C/15/Add.228, 2004), para. 42.

[153] CRC Committee, *Concluding Observations: Cameroon* (UN Doc. CRC/C/15/Add.164, 2001), para. 34.

[154] CRC Committee, *Concluding Observations: Colombia* (UN Doc. CRC/C/15/Add.137, 2000), para. 34.

[155] CRC Committee, *Concluding Observations: Argentina* (UN Doc. CRC/C/15/Add.187, 2002), para. 36.

[156] CRC Committee, *Concluding Observations: Guatemala* (UN Doc. CRC/C/15/Add.154, 2001), para. 54.

dealt with as violations of Article 6, which protects the child's right to life.[157] The Committee doesn't insist on a strict distinction between breaches of Article 6 and serious violations of Article 37(a), and in practice the two provisions inevitably overlap.

24. Some issues that are often subsumed within consideration of the issues of torture or other cruel, inhuman or degrading treatment or punishment do not appear to attract the consideration of the CRC Committee. Much of the contemporary international debate with respect to torture concerns its application in cases of *refoulement*. Countries, generally in the North, are accused of contributing to torture when they authorise the expulsion or deportation of individuals to countries where torture is a possibility. Human rights organisations argue that hollow and unsatisfactory 'diplomatic assurances' are being proffered to hide the likelihood of ill-treatment. Generally, however, cases of *refoulement* involve persons accused of terrorism or drug-related crimes, and it is perhaps for this reason that these issues do not seem to have confronted the Committee. They affect children indirectly, in that the expulsion of a parent to an unfriendly environment may have unhappy consequences for the child, and this raises the issue of what is in the child's best interests.

25. There are no references in the documentation of the CRC Committee to medical or scientific experimentation without the free consent of the person concerned. Although not mentioned explicitly in the CRC, the issue is dealt with in the second sentence of Article 7 of the CCPR. In its General Comment on Article 7, the Human Rights Committee noted that the reports of States Parties generally gave little or no information on this important point.[158] Surely it is of particular relevance with respect to children for whom issues of informed consent are of special significance.

3.1.3   *Corporal punishment*

26. Two specific forms of punishment, the death penalty and life imprisonment, are addressed in the second sentence of Article 37(a). However, the reference to 'torture or other cruel, inhuman or degrading treatment or punishment' invites consideration of other matters concerning punishment within the context of the first sentence of Article 37(a). It bears mention at the outset that the second sentence of the definition of torture in Article 1(1) of the Convention Against Torture states that torture 'does not include pain or suffering arising only from, inherent

---

[157] See in general M. Nowak, 'Article 6: The Right to Life', in: A. Alen, J. Vande Lanotte, E. Verhellen, F. Ang, E. Berghmans and M. Verheyde (eds.), *A Commentary on the United Nations Convention on the Rights of the Child* (Leiden, Martinus Nijhoff Publishers, 2005), para. 39.

[158] Human Rights Committee, Human Rights Committee, *General Comment No. 7: Torture or cruel, inhuman or degrading treatment or punishment (Art. 7)*, 1982, para. 3; Human Rights Committee, Human Rights Committee, *General Comment No. 20: Replaces general comment 7 concerning prohibition of torture and cruel treatment or punishment (Art. 7)*, 1992, para. 7.

in or incidental to lawful sanctions'. To the extent this definition applies to Article 37(a) of the Convention, it operates to limit the scope of the first sentence with respect to punishment imposed pursuant to lawful sanctions. For example, it would prevent life imprisonment, with or without the possibility of conditional release, being declared a form of torture or other cruel, inhuman or degrading treatment or punishment. This interpretation is further enhanced when the second sentence of Article 37(a) is used to limit the ambit of the first sentence.

The reference to 'lawful sanctions' in the definition of torture in the Convention Against Torture does not, as a matter of law, extend to 'other cruel, inhuman or degrading treatment or punishment', which is left undefined in the Convention. Indeed, the reference to 'punishment' suggests that it is under this rubric, rather than under that of torture, that 'punishment' associated with 'lawful sanctions' ought to be considered. The CRC Committee might therefore examine any forms of excessive or disproportionate punishments (with the stunning exception of the most severe of them all, life imprisonment), in its examination of Article 37(a). The concluding observations do not suggest that this has been an issue before the Committee, however. Its attention to the issue of 'punishment' is essentially confined to 'corporal punishment'.

27. Corporal punishment frequently occurs in detention centres and in schools, as well as within the family. According to the Human Rights Committee, the prohibition on torture and other cruel, inhuman or degrading treatment or punishment must extend to corporal punishment, including excessive chastisement as an educational or disciplinary measure.[159] The principle is also affirmed in the case law of the European Court of Human Rights.[160] In its General Comment on the right to education, the Committee on Economic, Social and Cultural Rights has said that 'corporal punishment is inconsistent with the fundamental guiding principle of international human rights law enshrined in the Preambles to the UDHR and both Covenants: the dignity of the individual'.[161] The CRC Committee has noted, in its own General Comment No. 1, that it 'has repeatedly made clear in its concluding observations that the use of corporal punishment does not respect the inherent dignity of the child nor the strict limits on school discipline'.[162]

---

[159] Human Rights Committee, Human Rights Committee, *General Comment No. 7: Torture or cruel, inhuman or degrading treatment or punishment (Art.7)*, 1982, para. 2. Also: Human Rights Committee, *General Comment No. 20: Replaces general comment 7 concerning prohibition of torture and cruel treatment or punishment (Art. 7)*, 1992, para. 5.
[160] ECtHR, *Tyrer* v. *United Kingdom*, 25 April 1978, Series A, No 26, (1979–80) 2 EHRR 1; ECtHR, *Campbell and Cosans* v. *United Kingdom*, 25 February 1982, Series A, No 48, (1982) 4 EHRR 293; ECtHR, *Costello-Roberts* v. *United Kingdom*, 25 March 1993, Series A, No 247-C.
[161] CESCR Committee, *General Comment No. 13 on the right to education* (UN Doc. E/C.12/1999/10, 1999), para. 41.
[162] CRC Committee, *General Comment No 1 on the Aims of Education* (UN Doc. CRC/GC/2001/1, 2001), para. para. 8.

In its consideration of Article 37(a), the Committee has drawn attention to the practice of corporal punishment, and there are other general references to the use of corporal punishment in the concluding observations on the Marshall Islands,[163] Kyrgyzstan,[164] Singapore,[165] Brunei Darussalam[166] and Sudan.[167] The Committee's concluding observations on Zambia note that there have been allegations of ill-treatment by law enforcement officers, 'despite the circular of 27 December 1999 ordering prison authorities to stop the practice of caning'.[168] In its discussion of Sierra Leone, the Committee 'urge[d] the State party to take legislative and educative measures to prohibit the use of corporal punishment by the courts, all public officials and in schools, and to consider the prohibition of its use in the family'.[169]

The Committee has also cited legislation that still allows corporal punishment, even if it pointed to no specific cases of implementation of the provisions. Thus, the Committee noted that in Dominica, children may be sentenced to 'whipping in private'.[170] The 1994 Juvenile Act in Qatar contemplates the possibility of flogging of persons under the age of eighteen.[171] The same concern was expressed with respect to the United Arab Emirates.[172] Similarly, the Committee referred to the existence of flogging as a lawful sanction in the 1977 Detention and Imprisonment Regulations in Saudi Arabia.[173] The Committee made no specific mention of Shariah law, but it did say it was disturbed that in Saudi Arabia certain sanctions, such as flogging, stoning and amputation, were 'systematically imposed by judicial authorities', although it gave no examples of this occurring with respect to young offenders.

---

[163] CRC Committee, *Concluding Observations: Marshall Islands* (UN Doc. CRC/C/15/Add.139, 2000), para. 36.

[164] CRC Committee, *Concluding Observations: Kyrgyzstan* (UN Doc. CRC/C/15/Add.127, 2000), para. 33.

[165] CRC Committee, *Concluding Observations: Singapore* (UN Doc. CRC/C/15/Add.220, 2003), para. 44.

[166] CRC Committee, *Concluding Observations: Brunei Darussalam* (UN Doc. CRC/C/15/Add.219, 2003), para. 55.

[167] CRC Committee, *Concluding Observations: Sudan* (UN Doc. CRC/C/15/Add.190, 2002), para. 35.

[168] CRC Committee, *Concluding Observations: Zambia* (UN Doc. CRC/C/15/Add.206, 2003), para. 32.

[169] CRC Committee, *Concluding Observations: Sierra Leone* (UN Doc. CRC/C/15/Add.116), para. 47. The Sierra Leone Truth and Reconciliation Commission, in its October 2004 report, recommended that corporal punishment of children in all of its forms be prohibited in Sierra Leone.

[170] CRC Committee, *Concluding Observations: Dominica* (UN Doc. CRC/C/15/Add.238, 2004), para. 46.

[171] CRC Committee, *Concluding Observations: Qatar* (UN Doc. CRC/C/15/Add.163, 2001), para. 43.

[172] CRC Committee, *Concluding Observations: United Arab Emirates* (UN Doc. CRC/C/15/Add.183, 2002), para. 32.

[173] CRC Committee, *Concluding Observations: Saudi Arabia* (UN Doc. CRC/C/15/Add.148, 2001), para. 33.

The Committee made virtually identical remarks with respect to Iran.[174] The Committee, like the other treaty bodies, normally uses diplomatic and euphemistic language. With respect to Saudi Arabia, however, it said bluntly: 'The Committee finds that application of such measures is incompatible with the Convention.'[175]

3.2   Death Penalty

28. The prohibition on execution for crimes committed by persons under the age of eighteen is extremely straightforward and leaves essentially no interpretative ambiguities. Within the overall logic of the CRC, this prohibition is of some interest and uniqueness, because as a general rule it applies to persons over the age of eighteen. Indeed, since the Convention was adopted, the rare recent cases of juveniles sentenced to death have concerned adolescents who offended when they were sixteen or seventeen years of age, but by the time that they had been tried and had exhausted their appeals, they have tended to be well into their twenties and even thirties.

29. The prohibition of execution of juvenile offenders is a feature of criminal justice that predates the Convention by many decades. It is really nothing more than a specific manifestation of the general rule establishing a threshold for criminal responsibility. The difficulty with the norm is that the age limit for execution varies, and historically, in some jurisdictions, it has been very low indeed. To take an example that today seems anomalous, as recently as the early 1960s Canadian courts sentenced to death a young offender who was fourteen at the time of the crime, and he was only saved from the noose as a result of executive clemency.[176] And in 1989, when Ireland finally ratified the CCPR, it formulated a reservation to Article 6(5), acknowledging that its legislation still allowed for execution of persons under the age of eighteen, although in the event of a death sentence imposed by a court, the executive would commute the sentence.

The real problem is therefore not with the prohibition of execution for crimes committed by young offenders, but rather with establishing the age to which this prohibition applies. On this point, in one of its very early contentious cases, the Inter-American Commission on Human Rights noted that there was no argument even about the existence of a customary legal norm prohibiting juvenile execution.[177] The real issue was whether it prohibited them for persons *under the age of eighteen,* and here the Commission said it could not conclude that such a norm existed,[178] a position it later reversed.[179] That such matters remain difficult is demon-

---

[174] *Ibid.*

[175] CRC Committee, *Concluding Observations: Iran* (UN Doc. CRC/C/15/Add.123, 2000), para. 37.

[176] J. Sher, *'Until You are Dead', Steven Truscott's Long Ride into History* (Toronto, Vintage Canada, 2002).

[177] Inter-American Commission on Human Rights, *Roach & Pinkerton* v. *United States, o.c.* (note 22), para. 56.

[178] *Ibid.,* para. 60.

[179] Inter-American Commission on Human Rights, *Domingues* v. *United States, o.c.* (note 22).

strated by the inability of the CRC itself to establish a general age threshold of criminal responsibility for children. Hence, the significance of the prohibition on the death penalty for crimes committed while under the age of eighteen, a norm that has been an almost uncontroversial standard in international human rights law since its incorporation in the CCPR in 1966.

30. It may be worth dwelling briefly on the debates surrounding the incorporation of the prohibition in the CCPR in order to understand the origins of this norm. The issue of juvenile executions had barely arisen in the early years when the draft Covenant was being prepared by the Commission on Human Rights. The Commission draft contained a prohibition on the execution of pregnant women, but said nothing about young offenders.[180] In the final version of the Covenant, the two categories appear in the same provision. It was during the debates in the Third Committee, in 1957, that the norm on juvenile executions was added. Amendments were proposed by Japan and Guatemala.[181] Japan submitted an amendment by which the Covenant would prohibit sentence of death 'on minors',[182] saying it was aimed at protecting the lives of children and young persons, who already enjoyed special protection pursuant to the draft economic, social, and cultural rights covenant.[183] Japan criticized a companion amendment on the subject, submitted by Guatemala,[184] that suggested the death penalty could be imposed after a young offender had attained the age of majority.[185] Finland seems to be at the origin of the suggestion that the provision make specific reference to persons under eighteen, arguing that this was also the age used in the fourth Geneva Convention.[186] A Working Party of the Committee attempted to reach a compromise, there was no agreement on the proper formulation, and three alternatives were considered: 'minors', 'persons below eighteen years of age', and 'juveniles'. For no apparent reason, the chair suggested that the Committee vote first on the phrase 'persons below eighteen years of age'.[187] It was adopted in a very close vote,[188] with the result that the alternatives were never considered. It is surely of interest that the prohibition of juvenile executions was not even included in the Commission on Human Rights draft of the

---

[180] UN Doc. E/2256, UN Doc. E/2447, UN Doc. A/2929. Suggestions that such a prohibition might be included had been made on occasion in the Commission, but never crystallized into a proposed amendment: UN Doc. E/CN.4/SR.139, para. 28; UN Doc. E/CN.4/384.

[181] UN Doc. A/C.3/L.647: 'Sentence of death shall not be carried out on minors or on a pregnant woman'. This amendment was later withdrawn: UN Doc. A/C.3/SR.816, para. 19.

[182] UN Doc. A/C.3/L.655 and Corr. 1: 'Sentence of death shall not be imposed for crimes committed by minors, and shall not be carried out on children and young persons or on a pregnant woman.'

[183] UN Doc. A/C.3/SR.814, para. 19.

[184] UN Doc. A/C.3/L.647: 'Sentence of death shall not be carried out on minors or on a pregnant woman'. This amendment was later withdrawn: UN Doc. A/C.3/SR.816, para. 19.

[185] Ibid., para. 19.

[186] UN Doc. A/C.3/SR.819, para. 10.

[187] Ibid., para. 19.

[188] Ibid., para. 21, by twenty one votes to nineteen, with twenty eight abstentions.

of the accused person, rather than any question as to whether Chinese law prohibits the practice.[204]

36. In Pakistan, a Christian, illiterate boy of twelve years of age was charged with blasphemy together with two adult men in 1993. After one of the men had been murdered by Muslim fundamentalists, the two remaining defendants were sentenced to death. Both were acquitted on appeal, but a mob that had gathered outside the courthouse demanded that they be put to death no matter what the sentence was. The men and the boy were forced to go into exile for safety reasons. When Pakistan's report indicated its legislation was compatible with the Convention, the Committee urged it to review this keeping in mind its concerns with such matters as the possible imposition of capital punishment for crimes committed under the age of eighteen.[205] Pakistan's representatives failed to answer a challenge that its laws were inconsistent with Article 37(a).[206] In 2000, Pakistan set the minimum age for the death penalty at the age of eighteen at the time of the offence, in accordance with Article 37(a). However, there has been some resistance to the Ordinance in the State. The Committee expressed concern that juveniles were, despite the promulgation of the Ordinance, being sentenced to death and executed,[207] and in 2004, the Punjab province's Lahore High Court annulled the law, blaming it for a rise in crime among young people.

37. Examining Nigeria's report, the Committee noted that it was possible for children to be sentenced to death, in violation of Article 37(a).[208] Nigeria indicated that its present legislation only limits the death penalty to seventeen, but that a draft decree will increase this to eighteen.[209] In Yemen a thirteen-year-old boy and three men were hanged on 21 July 1993, after having been convicted of murder and robbery. Yemen raised the minimum age for execution to eighteen at the time of the offence in 1994. However, the periodic reports of Yemen have seemed to suggest that persons over fifteen can be executed,[210] and its answers on this point have appeared evasive.[211] In its concluding observations on the Democratic Republic of the Congo, the Committee noted its concern that children aged sixteen or more

---

[204] Amnesty International, *Stop Child Executions! Ending the Death Penalty for Child Offenders* (AI Index: ACT 50/015/2004).
[205] CRC Committee, *Concluding Observations: Pakistan* (UN Doc. CRC/C/15/Add.18, 1994), para. 23.
[206] UN Doc. CRC/C/SR.133, para. 11.
[207] CRC Committee, *Concluding Observations: Pakistan* (UN Doc. CRC/C/15/Add.217, 2003), para. 80.
[208] CRC Committee, *Concluding Observations: Nigeria* (UN Doc. CRC/C/15/Add.61, 1996), paras. 20, 39 and(UN Doc. CRC/C/SR.323), paras. 56, 73, 84.
[209] UN Doc. CRC/C/SR.323, 1996, para. 73.
[210] CRC Committee, *Second periodic report of Yemen* (CRC/C/70/Add.1, 1998), para. 82(g).
[211] CRC/C/SR.262, 1996; CRC/C/SR.523, 1999, para. 28.

can be sentenced to death, although it recognised that a presidential pardon had recently been accorded in such cases.[212]

38. In its latest report to the CRC Committee, Saudi Arabia said capital punishment could not be imposed upon children 'who have not attained the age of majority in accordance with Islamic law'.[213] In its concluding observations on Saudi Arabia, the Committee stated: '[a]s the age of majority is not defined, the Committee is seriously concerned that there is a possibility that the death penalty may be imposed for offences committed by persons who were below 18 years at the time the crime was committed, contrary to Articles 6 and 37 (a) of the Convention.'[214] Hence, the Committee 'strongly recommend[ed] that the State party take immediate steps to halt and abolish by law the imposition of the death penalty for crimes committed by persons under 18'.[215]

39. Iran is the only State where the practice of juvenile executions overtly continues. Yet, Iran is party to the Convention; and the Committee has observed succinctly: 'In light of articles 6 and 37 (a) of the Convention, the Committee is seriously disturbed at the applicability of the death penalty for crimes committed by persons under 18 and emphasizes that such a penalty is incompatible with the Convention.'[216] Still, however, as recently as December 2004, there were media reports of a twenty-two-year-old due to be executed 'in the next few days' for killing a member of the security forces when he was seventeen.[217] And there have also been reports that in September 2004, a sixteen-year-old Afghan boy was sentenced to death in Karaz, Iran, for involvement in a drug trafficking scheme.

40. Since 1985, the United States has executed the largest number of people for crimes committed before the age of eighteen (with the possible exceptions of Iran and Iraq, where official statistics are not to be trusted). As of 1 March 2005, nineteen state jurisdictions had legislation permitting the practice. In recent years, juvenile offenders were executed in Oklahoma, Texas and Virginia. Nevertheless, the practice of executing young offenders in the United States had been in steady decline. In 2003, only two sentences were imposed, compared with fifteen in 1999. In 1988, in *Thompson v. Oklahoma*, the United States Supreme Court held that executions of offenders aged fifteen and younger at the time of their crimes would be unconstitutional. Several states have also recently enacted legislation to prohibit executions for crimes committed while under the age of eighteen. In 1989, a

---

[212] CRC Committee, *Concluding Observations: Democratic Republic of the Congo* (UN Doc. CRC/C/15/Add.153, 2001), para. 74.

[213] CRC Committee, *Initial Report of Saudi Arabia* (UN Doc. CRC/C/61/Add.2, 2000), para. 253.

[214] CRC Committee, *Concluding Observations: Saudi Arabia* (UN Doc. CRC/C/15/Add.148, 2001), para. 27 and(UN Doc. CRC/C/SR.688, 2001), para. 42.

[215] *Ibid.*

[216] CRC Committee, *Concluding Observations: Iran* (UN Doc. CRC/C/15/Add.123, 2000), para. 29.

[217] See: http://www.iranfocus.com/modules/news/article.php?storyid=1108

constitutional challenge to the practice failed by only one vote.[218] Sixteen years later, undoubtedly driven by international developments and an acknowledgement of universal consensus on the subject, the United States Supreme Court reversed itself. On 1 March 2005, a five-judge majority of the Court ruled that execution of persons for crimes committed under the age of eighteen was unconstitutional, and contrary to the eighth amendment to the Constitution. According to the majority,

> A majority of States have rejected the imposition of the death penalty on juvenile offenders under 18, and we now hold this is required by the Eighth Amendment. [...] Our determination that the death penalty is disproportionate punishment for offenders under 18 finds confirmation in the stark reality that the United States is the only country in the world that continues to give official sanction to the juvenile death penalty. This reality does not become controlling, for the task of interpreting the Eighth Amendment remains our responsibility. Yet at least from the time of the Court's decision in *Trop*, the Court has referred to the laws of other countries and to international authorities as instructive for its interpretation of the Eighth Amendment's prohibition of cruel and unusual punishments.[219]

The judgment acknowledges the applicable international standards, including Article 37(a) of the Convention on the Rights of the Child.

3.3   Life Imprisonment

41. An unfortunate compromise that was made in the final moments of the drafting of Article 37(a) allows for the possibility that children will be sentenced to life imprisonment and never released. Although the text speaks about the 'possibility of release', this may well be subject to severe restrictions and even arbitrary discretionary authority. This has been the case in the United Kingdom, where individuals well into adulthood continue to serve life sentences for crimes committed while adolescents. They are sentenced to detention 'at her Majesty's pleasure', which means that periodic review of such indefinite detention is undertaken on a purely discretionary basis. In *Hussain v. United Kingdom*,[220] the European Court of Human Rights looked at the absence of a right of judicial review in the United Kingdom for detained former juvenile criminals, and stated: 'A failure to have regard to the changes that inevitably occur with maturation would mean that young persons detained under section 53 would be treated as having forfeited their liberty for the rest of their lives, a situation which, as the applicant and the Delegate of the Commission pointed out, might give rise to questions under Article 3 (Article 3) of the [*European Convention of Human Rights*].'[221] The Court also recognized that '[t]he decisive ground for the applicant's continued detention was and continues to be

---

[218] *Stanford* v. *Kentucky; Wilkins* v. *Missouri*, 492 U.S. 361, 109 S.Ct. 2969 (1989). Also: *Thompson* v. *Oklahoma*, 487 U.S. 815, 108 S.Ct. 2687, 101 L.Ed.2d 702 (1988).
[219] *Roper* v. *Simmons*, 543 US ____ (2005), paras. 11 and 16 (reference omitted).
[220] ECtHR, *Hussain* v. *United Kingdom*, 21 February 1996, *E.C.H.R.* 8, 1996.
[221] *Ibid.*, para. 53.

his dangerousness to society, a characteristic susceptible to change with the passage of time'.[222] The Court affirmed that the detainee had the right to take proceedings to have his sentence reviewed by a court periodically.[223]

The CRC Committee has criticised other States with similar legislation, notably Zambia[224] and Dominica.[225] However, in its Initial State Report, Zambia explained that a sentence 'at the president's pleasure' left open 'a possibility of release in that the President can exercise the prerogative of mercy at any time'.[226] Zambia considered itself to be in compliance with Article 37(a).

42. There is relatively little to be found in the consideration of periodic reports on the issue of life imprisonment. Most States, such as Romania[227] and Kazakhstan,[228] clearly state their compliance to the life imprisonment provisions of the Convention. Israel has reported that life imprisonment of juveniles is present in its legislation: 'the Supreme Court ruled that if a court finds it appropriate to impose a life prison sentence in certain circumstances, it may do so, even with respect to a minor'.[229] Yet, the Committee did not bring up Israel's default under the Convention, instead vaguely advising Israel to '[e]nsure that the provisions of the Convention, in particular Articles 37, 39 and 40, are fully integrated into the legislation and practice of [its] system of juvenile justice'.[230] In one of its periodic reports, Sudan expressed non-compliance with its Convention obligations: 'Article 33, paragraph 3, of the Penal Code of 1991 stipulates that, except for crimes of brigandry, a sentence of life imprisonment may not be handed down to any person under 18 years of age.'[231] The Committee was more direct with Sudan than with Israel, asking 'that sentences of life imprisonment without possibility of release are . . . not handed down'.[232]

A substantial problem with respect to life imprisonment, however, appears to come when States try juveniles as adults, thus allowing for the possibility that the adult sentence of life imprisonment will be imposed on these juveniles. With respect to Burkina Faso, for example, the Committee found itself 'deeply concerned at the possibility that children of 16 and 17 years of age are treated like adults and can

---

[222] *Ibid.*, para. 54.

[223] *Ibid.*, paras. 47–48.

[224] CRC Committee, *Concluding Observations: Zambia* (UN Doc. CRC/C/15/Add.206, 2003), para. 72.

[225] CRC Committee, *Concluding Observations: Dominica* (UN Doc. CRC/C/15/Add.238, 2004), para. 46.

[226] CRC Committee, *Initial report of Zambia* (UN Doc. CRC/C/11/Add.25), para. 551.

[227] CRC Committee, *Second periodic report of Romania* (UN Doc. CRC/C/65/Add.19), para. 169.

[228] CRC Committee, *Initial report of Kasakhstan* (UN Doc. CRC/C/41/Add.13), para. 337.

[229] CRC Committee, *Periodic report of Israel* (UN Doc. CRC/C/8/Add.44), para. 416 (citing *Criminal Appeal 530/90 Anonymous Plaintiff v. State of Israel*, P.D. 46(3) 652).

[230] CRC Committee, *Concluding Observations: Israel* (UN Doc. CRC/C/15/Add.195, 2002), para. 63(a).

[231] CRC Committee, *Second periodic report of Sudan* (UN Doc. CRC/C/65/Add.17), para. 42.

[232] CRC Committee, *Concluding Observations: Sudan* (UN Doc. CRC/C/15/Add.190, 2002), para. 70(d).

be subjected to . . . life imprisonment, which is a serious violation of Article 37 of the Convention'.[233] Japan was equally of concern to the Committee, as an 'increasing number of juveniles are tried as adults and sentenced to detention, and that juveniles may be sentenced to life imprisonment'.[234]

---

[233] CRC Committee, *Concluding Observations: Burkina Faso* (UN Doc. CRC/C/15/Add.193, 2002), para. 60.

[234] CRC Committee, *Concluding Observations: Japan* (UN Doc. CRC/C/15/Add.231, 2004), para. 53.

PART II   DEPRIVATION OF LIBERTY OF CHILDREN
(ARTICLE 37(b), (c), (d))

Helmut Sax

CHAPTER ONE

INTRODUCTION*

43. 'Every social problem has a corresponding detention structure'—a rather polemical statement[235] which nevertheless summarizes still widely prevailing approaches in policy and public opinion on deprivation of liberty in general, but also, more specifically, in relation to children. In many countries children[236] continue to be arrested, detained, even imprisoned for petty crimes; asylum-seeking children may spend months in administrative detention pending their deportation; children are placed in closed custodial institutions under inadequate child welfare regimes—it is estimated that more than one million children are deprived of their liberty world-

---

* March 2005. The author wishes to thank Dagmar Koblischke and Beatrix Ferenci for their valuable research support to this contribution.

[235] Statement by Emilio Garcia Mendez, Children and Juveniles in Detention, in: Children in Trouble—Children and Juveniles in Detention: Application of Human Rights Standards, United Nations Expert Group Meeting, Vienna/Austria (30th October–4th November 1994), Austrian Federal Ministry for Youth and Family, Vienna 1995, 105; the statement was made with particular reference to the correctional doctrines of the 19th century and their continuing impact on Latin American approaches to child offenders.

[236] A note here on terminology and the use of the term 'child': Within the context of deprivation of liberty reference is frequently made to the 'juvenile', instead of the 'child', mostly in relation to a criminal/juvenile justice background. However, in the following discussion on Art 37(b), (c), (d), the author will generally remain with the notion 'child', for several reasons: firstly, because there is no consistence in the term 'juvenile' neither: compare Rule 2(2)(a) of the 1985 UN Standard Minimum Rules for the Administration of Juvenile Justice ('The Beijing Rules'), GA Res. 40/33 (29 November 1985) (hereafter: Beijing Rules): 'A juvenile is a child or young person who, under the respective legal systems, may be dealt with for an offence in a manner which is different from an adult'; to Rule 11(a) of the 1990 UN Rules for the Protection of Juveniles Deprived of their Liberty, GA Res. 45/113 (14 December 1990) (hereafter: JDL Rules), 'A juvenile is every person under the age of 18' (which also blurs any distinction from the definition of the 'child' in Art. 1 of the CRC). Secondly, for the sake of consistency in the general child rights discourse, which often refers to principles of 'child-sensitivity', 'child orientation' and the best interests of children, even in a more specific context addressing mainly older age groups (*cf.* the 1997 Guidelines for Action on Children in the Criminal Justice System, Annex to ECOSOC Res. 1997/30, 21 July 1997). Thirdly, and most importantly, the common understanding of a 'juvenile' still bears a strong connotation to criminal/juvenile justice, thus, hindering a broader and more openly discussion on deprivation of liberty in other settings.

wide.[237] Manifold reasons are given for restricting the personal liberty of children—public order and state security considerations, punishment, concerns of protection of others or even the child itself (*e.g.* in case of mental illness of children). It is against this background that over the last decades an increasingly comprehensive body of legal standards has evolved, which promotes child rights and child development-oriented approaches that do not consider young persons any more 'as mere objects of socialization and control'[238] and which call for any form of deprivation of liberty as a rare, exceptional measure only.[239]

44. No meeting of friends at school, no promising start of a job career, no support to the parents at home—depriving young persons of their regular family and social life, of educational opportunities, and, more basically, of choices simply to enter, stay or leave places at their own will, obviously has fundamental impact on the personal development as well as the exercise of human rights. Any form of deprivation of liberty seriously interferes with many other rights of the child concerned, such as the right to be cared for by the parents, access to education and health care, and leaves the child particularly vulnerable to violence and exploitation. Still, the CRC acknowledges the child as bearer of fundamental rights aimed at ensuring the 'full and harmonious development' of the child's personality and well-being[240] irrespective of the circumstances. And the UN JDL Rules stress the principle that '[j]uveniles deprived of their liberty shall not for any reason related to their status be denied the civil, economic, political, social or cultural rights to which they are entitled under national or international law, and which are compatible with the deprivation of liberty' (Rule 13). More specifically, aimed at imprisonment, the restrictions on personal liberty should be the sanction only, not any further infringements on other rights (*e.g.* by disregard to one's privacy, bad prison conditions, lack of education, vocational training).

45. Article 37(b), (c), (d) of the CRC on deprivation of liberty encompasses a broad range of standards, including for imposing such measures (lawful, non-arbitrary, measure of last resort and for shortest appropriate time only—lit (b)) as well as for

---

[237] UNICEF, *Justice for Children: Detention as a last Resort—Innovative Initiatives in the East Asia and Pacific Region* Bangkok 2004, 4.

[238] Para. 3 of the 1990 UN Guidelines for the Prevention of Juvenile Delinquency (Riyadh Guidelines), UN GA Resolution 45/112 (14 December 1990) (hereafter: Riyadh Guidelines).

[239] 'The new international legal philosophy aims to limit both the occasions and the periods of time for which liberty can be restricted', G. Van Bueren, *The International Law on the Rights of the Child* (The Hague, Martinus Nijhoff Publishers, 1998), p. 227.

[240] *Cf.* Articles 6 and 3(1), as well as the Preamble: 'Recognizing that the child, for the full and harmonious development of his or her personality, should grow up in a family environment, in an atmosphere of happiness, love and understanding'; and 'Considering that the child should be fully prepared to live an individual life in society and brought up in the spirit of the ideals proclaimed in the Charter of the United Nations, and in particular in the spirit of peace, dignity, tolerance, freedom, equality and solidarity, [. . .]'.

respect during such measures (adequate conditions and treatment of the child, separation from adults, contacts—lit (c); access to legal and other assistance, challenging legality of measure and prompt decision—lit (d)). Article 37(a) may be seen as providing important qualifications to these standards, prohibiting death penalty and life imprisonment without parole as a form of punishment and guaranteeing to the child protection from torture or other cruel, inhuman or degrading treatment or punishment.[241]

46. CRC standards on deprivation of liberty of children benefit from two distinct but related legal backgrounds: a strong civil rights foundation protecting personal liberty from arbitrary interferences which dates back to the times of the 1215 Magna Charta and other well-established principles on the national and international level,[242] and secondly, more recent developments of the 1980s especially in the juvenile justice field. At a first look, the similarities of Article 37 of the CRC and CCPR provisions are striking and may give the—misleading—impression of child rights standards being just another CRC-typical repetition of provisions found almost identically in other human rights treaties adopted well before the CRC. This would ignore, however, important additions to the CRC text not contained in any other treaty (like the 'last resort' clause) and the child-focussed set of other non-binding international standards, for which Article 37 of the CRC provides the main anchor and which bear direct relevance to interpretation of standards on deprivation of liberty of young persons (like the Beijing Rules and the JDL Rules). In fact, Article 37 standards on deprivation of liberty constitute a unique blend of general human rights norms, child rights concepts and criminal justice developments, a significant feature to be kept in mind for interpretation and implementation.

47. The drafting history of Article 37(b), (c), (d) shows that initially the discussion of deprivation of liberty was just one part of the discussion of CRC-related criminal justice matters. International developments at that time in related fields (Beijing Rules adopted; JDL Rules, Tokyo Rules,[243] Riyadh Guidelines under preparation) exerted significant influence on the drafting process. Moreover, not least the separation of articles into deprivation of liberty (now Article 37) on the one hand and juvenile justice (now Article 40) on the other may be seen as the first step towards an emancipation of deprivation of liberty from the bonds of the criminal justice context, leading to a more comprehensive approach which encompasses all kinds of restrictions of the child's personal liberty, no matter under which legal regime, and be it public or private. The practice of the CRC Committee as the principal authority for monitoring and interpreting the Convention has demonstrated its willingness to apply standards on deprivation of liberty beyond the confines of juvenile justice.

---

[241] *Cf. supra* Part I.
[242] *Cf.*, for instance, the Habeas Corpus Act of 1679; or Articles 3, 9 of the UDHR of 1948.
[243] United Nations Standard Minimum Rules for Non-custodial Measures 1990.

48. Mention should also be made here of the specific nature of standards contained in Article 37(b), (c), (d). Usually, CRC norms focus on an individual's right (to health, for instance); here, however, provisions actually highlight less the protected right—personal liberty of the child, which is not even mentioned by the CRC[244]—but the standards to be respected for interference with this right, reducing them primarily to procedural guarantees. This is relevant insofar as the right to personal liberty has never been seen as an absolute right (like the prohibition of slavery), more to the contrary: deprivation of liberty is used by almost all societies as a legitimate form of sanction. In the CRC's child development-focussed context, however, the values of the right to personal liberty itself come to the forefront again. Consequently, CRC standards on deprivation of liberty and related international standards require more substantive considerations beyond procedural matters, including discussion of alternative measures to deprivation of liberty and institutionalisation.[245]

49. As an example, a juvenile justice system challenges the rather routinely recourse to imprisonment as a sanction. Once it is accepted that non-compliance by the growing child with norms and standards of the adult world is—within certain limits—part of the regular development process,[246] not necessarily requiring full-fledged criminal justice responses, then justification for deprivation of liberty as the strongest instrument of the traditional sanction regime is lost. Hence, the need for alternatives: to deprivation of liberty (*e.g.* community services) or to the formal justice system as a whole (through diversion, *e.g.* focus on conflict resolution, restorative justice mechanisms). The same approach is true for other contexts as well—today, 'correction' of 'difficult children' by means of locking them up in closed 'educational institutions' is generally not regarded any more as an appropriate social reaction. In the end, standards on deprivation of liberty, in particular the last resort clause, in combination with concerns about the negative impact of institutionalisation of children do call into question any policy of segregation and referral to closed institutions of children not complying with mainstream standards of 'normalcy' and 'adaptation'. And ultimately, a discussion on the child's personal liberty and justification for its deprivation through private actors, in the private sphere, including the family, is urgently needed. Above all, a certain favourable political and societal setting for implementation of CRC standards on deprivation of liberty is required, which is in fact missing in most countries, as the practice of the CRC Committee highlights.[247] Unfortunately, the Committee's own work often

---

[244] *Cf.*, the explicit reference in Art 9 ICCPR: 'Everyone has the right to liberty and security of the person'.

[245] *Cf.* in this regard, the 2004 Recommendation No. 7 of the CRC Committee on Children without parental care.

[246] *Cf.* Rule 5e of the Beijing Rules.

[247] In relation to juvenile justice: 'Noting that the experience of the Committee in its review of reports presented by States parties on their implementation of the Convention on the Rights of the Child has shown that in all regions of the world and in relation to all legal

lacks of a distinct, consistent focus on deprivation of liberty outside the traditional juvenile justice context. This is particularly regrettable as there is no other comparably well-suited international monitoring body to oversee implementation of standards on deprivation of liberty of children, including the JDL Rules.[248]

---

systems, the provisions of the Convention relating to the administration of juvenile justice are in many instances not reflected in national legislation or practice, giving cause for serious concern', CRC Committee, *Recommendation No. 2 on the Administration of Juvenile Justice* (UN Doc. CRC/C/90, 1999), p. 3. *Cf.* also the assessment of political motives behind State disregard of juvenile justice in B. Abramson, *Juvenile Justice: The unwanted child of state responsibilities—Compilation and analysis of Concluding Observations on Juvenile Justice issues, UN Committee on the Rights of the Child, 1993—January 2000* (Geneva, International Network on Juvenile Justice/Defence for Children International, 2000).

[248] *Cf.* G. Van Bueren, *o.c.* (note 239), p. 211.

CHAPTER TWO

COMPARISON WITH RELATED INTERNATIONAL
HUMAN RIGHTS PROVISIONS

1. *Universal Standards*

50. As one of the oldest human rights, Article 37(b), (c), (d) of the CRC can draw on several predecessors in formulating guarantees on deprivation of liberty. The CRC drafting history clearly reveals the close link between the various treaties, especially as far as the CCPR is concerned. In the following, aspects of this relationship will be examined, complemented by exemplary references to other treaties, non-binding instruments and relevant mechanisms based on the UN Charter and the work of the UN Commission on Human Rights.

51. A comparison of relevant provisions on deprivation of liberty of the 1948 UDHR and the 1966 CCPR to the 1989 CRC demonstrates clear congruencies, including (partly identical) wording, but also significant divergence in some aspects. While Articles 3 and 9 of the UDHR simply provide for the basic guarantees of the individual's right 'to liberty and security of the person' and the general prohibition of arbitrary deprivation of liberty, the CCPR further elaborates on these standards. Article 9 of the CCPR adds requirements of lawfulness, specific rights upon arrest and criminal charges, release on bail, 'habeas corpus' proceedings for review of the legality of the deprivation of liberty and a right to compensation for unlawful arrest or detention. Furthermore, Article 10 introduces a set of standards on conditions and treatment during deprivation of liberty, including treatment 'with humanity and respect for the inherent dignity of the human person',[249] the separation of accused persons from already convicted inmates, the separation of juveniles from adults at all stages and, finally, the stated objective of penitentiary systems to promote reformation and social rehabilitation of prisoners.

52. The CRC selectively extracts and merges many of these guarantees of Articles 9 and 10 of the CCPR in one single Article 37.[250] In terms of omission, however, the CRC text contains no explicit reference to the right to liberty and security of the

---

[249] Thereby extending the right to personal integrity beyond the confines of the prohibition of torture or cruel, inhuman or degrading treatment or punishment, as contained in Article 7 of the CCPR.

[250] With the additional inclusion of the prohibition of torture, capital punishment and life sentence without parole for juvenile offenders, in Article 37(a).

UDHR and the CCPR, no information rights upon arrest, no right to be brought promptly before a judge or other competent officer and no right to compensation.[251] Yet this must not be regarded as a restriction of standards in relation to children and juveniles. Considering the drafting process of Article 37, it has not been the intention of the drafters to simply repeat in the CRC context the already existing body of standards on deprivation of liberty;[252] the relationship between the CCPR (and the International Bill of Rights at large) and the CRC are of a complementary nature. Furthermore, the savings clause of Article 41 of the CRC upholds any provisions of international law 'which are more conducive to the realization of the rights of the child'.[253]

53. Following from the above, the CCPR right to compensation for unlawful arrest or detention, for instance, should not be overlooked in the CRC context as well.[254] Furthermore, while the CRC does not repeat the express reference of Article 3 of the UDHR and Article 9(1) of the CCPR to the right to security of the person as linked to personal liberty, the right to security bears relevance for the context of deprivation of liberty of children, particularly in regard to interferences by private persons as a horizontal effect of this right.[255]

54. Further human rights treaty provisions of importance in situations of deprivation of liberty of children include the 1966 International Covenant on Economic, Social and Cultural Rights,[256] the 1979 Convention on the Elimination of All Forms of Discrimination against Women,[257] the 1965 International Convention on the

---

[251] Guarantees of due process and the aims of juvenile criminal justice are addressed by Article 40 of the CRC. See G. Van Bueren, 'Article 40: The Administration of Juvenile Justice', in: A. Alen, J. Vande Lanotte, E. Verhellen, F. Ang, E. Berghmans and M. Verheyde (eds.), o.c. (note 157).

[252] As the Representative of Austria has stated, 'care should be taken not to include the provisions of other existing international human rights instruments already applicable to children', UN Doc. E/CN.4/1986/39, 1986, para. 91; reproduced in S. Detrick (ed.), A Guide to the 'Travaux préparatoires' (Dordrecht—Boston—London, Martinus Nijhoff Publishers, 1992), p. 462.

[253] S. Detrick, A Commentary on the United Nations Convention on the Rights of the Child (The Hague—Boston—London, Martinus Nijhoff Publishers, 1999), p. 713, with further references.

[254] Provided that the respective State is Party to both treaties. Similarly, Article 11 of the CCPR excludes—although with limited relevance in the context of children—the imprisonment of young persons 'merely on the grounds of inability to fulfil a contractual obligation'.

[255] One could think of situations of intimidations and threats against young persons, attempts of abduction and disappearance; for a discussion of the distinct content of the right to personal security vis-à-vis personal liberty, cf. M. Nowak, UN Covenant on Civil and Political Rights—CCPR Commentary (second edition, Kehl-Strasbourg-Arlington, N.P. Engel Publishers, 2005), Article 9, para. 8, with reference to the case of Delgado Paéz v. Colombia before the Human Rights Committee in 1990 and further case law.

[256] Cf., e.g., the right to work, vocational training and fair conditions of work (Articles 6, 7).

[257] Cf., e.g., Art 15(1) and (2) on equality of women and men before the law and in courts at all stages.

Elimination of All Forms of Racial Discrimination,[258] and the 1990 International Convention on the Protection of the Rights of All Migrant Workers and Members of Their Families, which provides for a broad set of guarantees on deprivation of liberty in relation to 'migrant workers and members of their families'.[259]

55. Special mention should be made here of the protection offered by the 2002 Optional Protocol to the 1984 Convention against Torture and other Cruel, Inhuman or Degrading Treatment or Punishment. The purpose of this new mechanism is to 'establish a system of regular visits undertaken by independent international and national bodies to places where people are deprived of their liberty, in order to prevent torture and other cruel, inhuman or degrading treatment or punishment' (Article 1). Concerning the definition of the term 'deprivation of liberty' it is interesting to note that the Optional Protocol (Article 4(2)) uses in almost identical wording the definition contained in Rule 11(b) of the JDL Rules. Consequently, in relation to places of detention falling under the scope of the Protocol, Article 4(1) states that each 'State Party shall allow visits, in accordance with the present Protocol, by the mechanisms referred to in articles 2 and 3 to any place under its jurisdiction and control where persons are or may be deprived of their liberty, either by virtue of an order given by a public authority or at its instigation or with its consent or acquiescence'. The visiting mechanism should provide far-reaching support to prevention of ill-treatment of children deprived of their liberty through independent monitoring, not limited to places of detention under the criminal/juvenile justice regime only but including also, *e.g.* custodial institutions in a youth welfare setting.

56. In terms of non-treaty standards on children deprived of their liberty and their relevance for CRC interpretation it should be observed that a typical set of CRC Committee recommendations under the State reporting procedure does not only refer to relevant Articles 37, 40 and 39, but also to 'other United Nations standards in this field' (see also Article 40(2)), such as the:

– Beijing Rules,
– Riyadh Guidelines,
– JDL Rules[260]
– Guidelines for Action on Children in the Criminal Justice System, 1997.[261]

---

[258] *Cf.*, *e.g.*, Article 5(a) and (b) on equality before courts and the right to security without racial discrimination.

[259] See Articles 16 and 17, based on CCPR articles 9 and 10, but further elaborated.

[260] The before-mentioned standards are all reproduced in G. van Bueren (ed.), *International Documents on Children* (Dordrecht—Boston—London, Martinus Nijhoff Publishers, 1993), p. 199 *et seq.* For a brief overview of these standards, *cf.* also, R. Krech, 'UN Crime Prevention', in: Eugeen Verhellen (ed.), *Understanding Children's Rights* (Ghent, Children's Rights Centre/ University of Ghent, 1996), pp. 373–384.

[261] Recommended by Economic and Social Council resolution 1997/30 of 21 July 1997, Annex.

57. Most of these child-focussed standards have been worked out within the UN criminal justice and crime prevention framework (UN Commission on Crime Prevention and Criminal Justice, United Nations Office on Drugs and Crime). They are further complemented by UN instruments generally applicable in the context of deprivation of liberty of all persons, including the:

– Standard Minimum Rules for the Treatment of Prisoners, 1955,
– Code of Conduct for Law Enforcement Officials, 1979,
– Principles of Medical Ethics relevant to the Role of Health Personnel, particularly Physicians, in the Protection of Prisoners and Detainees against Torture and Other Cruel, Inhuman or Degrading Treatment or Punishment, 1982,
– Body of Principles for the Protection of All Persons under Any Form of Detention or Imprisonment, 1988,
– Principles on the Effective Prevention and Investigation of Extra-legal, Arbitrary and Summary Executions, 1989,
– Basic Principles for the Treatment of Prisoners, 1990,
– United Nations Standard Minimum Rules for Non-custodial Measures (The Tokyo Rules), 1990,
– Declaration on the Protection of All Persons from Enforced Disappearance, 1992.[262]

58. As far as States Parties obligations to protect children from arbitrary deprivation of liberty through private persons are concerned, the following standards elaborated in the framework of the Hague Conference on Private International Law should also taken into consideration (*e.g.* in cases of child abduction, international adoption, monitoring of placement of children, custodial responsibilities for refugee children):[263]

– Convention on the Civil Aspects of International Child Abduction, 1980,
– Convention on Protection of Children and Co-operation in respect of Intercountry Adoption, 1993,
– Convention on Jurisdiction, Applicable Law, Recognition, Enforcement and Co-Operation in Respect of Parental Responsibility and Measures for the Protection of Children, 1996.

59. Another important avenue of developing standards on deprivation of liberty on the universal level relates to the activities of the UN Commission on Human

---

[262] *Cf.* Article 10(1): Any person deprived of liberty shall be held in an officially recognized place of detention and, in conformity with national law, be brought before a judicial authority promptly after detention. Article 20(1): States shall prevent and suppress the abduction of children of parents subjected to enforced disappearance and of children born during their mother's enforced disappearance, and shall devote their efforts to the search for and identification of such children and to the restitution of the children to their families of origin.

[263] *Cf.* also the UN Declaration on Social and Legal Principles relating to the Protection and Welfare of Children, with Special Reference to Foster Placement and Adoption Nationally and Internationally, 1986.

Rights (CHR) and its thematic and country-specific mandates (through Working Groups, Special Rapporteurs, Independent Experts). In the discharge of their mandate many of them have to deal with situations of children deprived of their personal liberty, concerning, for example, harassment of street children or child prostitutes, mandatory detention of child refugees or access to education in detention. However, the level of attention by these mechanisms accorded specifically to children varies to a considerable degree.

60. The UN Working Group on Arbitrary Detention was set up in 1991 by Commission on Human Rights Resolution 1991/42; its five independent expert members are 'entrusted with the task of investigating cases of deprivation of liberty imposed arbitrarily, provided that no final decision has been taken in such cases by domestic courts in conformity with domestic law, with the relevant international standards set forth in the UDHR and with the relevant international instruments accepted by the States concerned'.[264] The Working Group considers cases as 'arbitrary detention' when falling in one of the following 'categories':

- deprivation of liberty, 'when it is clearly impossible to invoke any legal basis justifying the deprivation of liberty',
- deprivation of liberty as a result from the exercise of selective political rights and freedoms (*e.g.* freedom of expression, of religion) and rights to equality contained in the UDHR and the CCPR,
- total or partial non-observance of international fair trial standards 'of such gravity as to give the deprivation of liberty an arbitrary character'.[265]

61. As far as children are concerned, the Working Group has had to deal with deprivation of liberty of the child in various situations, but so far, it has not adopted specific general recommendations or deliberations on children.[266] Still, according to its Revised Methods of Work[267] the Group's body of reference standards explicitly includes the JDL Rules and the Beijing Rules. The Working Group may also adopt 'Opinions' on individual cases of arbitrary detention, which has included in the past violations of standards in relation to personal liberty of the child.[268] It is important to note that since 1997 both the Commission of Human Rights and the Working Group generally use the broader term 'deprivation of liberty' in respect to their activities (instead of 'detention', without changing the name of the Group, however) and expressly clarified its mandate to include administrative custody of

---

[264] Commission on Human Rights resolution 2000/36, clarifying the mandate based on Resolutions 1991/42 of 5 March 1991 and 1997/50 of 15 April 1997.

[265] UN Doc. E/CN.4/1998/44 (19 December 1997), Annex 1, para. 8.

[266] The statistics of cases regularly contained in the annex to the annual reports of the Group are disaggregated by sex only, but not by age groups.

[267] Contained in UN Doc. E/CN.4/1998/44 (19 December 1997), Annex 1.

[268] *E.g.*, Opinion No. 19/2000 (China) concerning two young Tibetan monks, UN Doc. E/CN.4/2001/14/Add.1 (9 November 2000).

asylum-seekers and immigrants.[269] In this regard, the Group also undertook several country visits, assessing the situation of asylum-seekers deprived of their liberty, including children: in its 'Conclusions and Recommendations' to the Government of the United Kingdom, the Working Group frankly stated: 'Unaccompanied minors should never be detained.'[270] Similarly critical comments were addressed to the Government of Australia after its visit in 2002.[271]

62. Other CHR mechanisms of relevance for the protection of children from violations of their rights to personal liberty and security include the activities of the Working Group on Enforced or Involuntary Disappearances,[272] the Special Rapporteur on extra-judicial, summary or arbitrary executions,[273] the Special Rapporteur on the question of torture and other cruel, inhuman or degrading treatment or punishment,[274] the Special Rapporteur on violence against women, its causes and consequences,[275] the Special Rapporteur on the sale of children, child prostitution and child pornography,[276] the Special Rapporteur on the right of everyone to the enjoy-

---

[269] Commission on Human Rights resolution 1997/50 (15 April 1997), para. 4.

[270] *Report on the visit of the Working Group to the United Kingdom on the issue of immigrants and asylum seekers* (UN Doc. E/CN.4/1999/63/Add.3, 1998), para. 37.

[271] 'The system of mandatory detention sets up a presumption whereby each unlawful non-citizen, if not detained, represents a danger to the community, even in cases when the implementation of this system results in the detention of children, elderly or sick people and others in a vulnerable situation, the detention of whom is obviously not absolutely necessary to achieve the aims of the immigration policy', *Report of the Working Group, visit to Australia* (UN Doc. E/CN.4/2003/8/Add.2, 2002), para. 13.

[272] In its 2004 report (UN Doc. E/CN.4/2004/58, 2004), the Group dealt with cases of disappeared children in Argentina, Ecuador, El Salvador, India and Zimbabwe. Apart from that drafting of a legally binding convention on enforced disappearances has started in 2001, and M. Nowak, was charged as an 'independent expert' with examining the existing international criminal and human rights framework for the protection of persons from enforced or involuntary disappearances; *cf.* his report, which includes analysis both in regard to personal liberty and the protection of children and the recommendation to improved protection through a legally binding document, UN Doc. E/CN.4/2002/71, 2002.

[273] *Cf. e.g.* references to children in UN Docs. E/CN.4/2004/7, 2003 and E/CN.4/1999/39, 1999.

[274] *Cf. e.g.* Interim report of the Special Rapporteur of the Commission on Human Rights on the question of torture and other cruel, inhuman or degrading treatment or punishment, UN Doc. A/55/290, 2000, para. 10, on special issues of concern, including 'torture and children': 'The resulting lack of appropriate attention to the medical, emotional, educational, rehabilitative and recreational needs of detained children can result in conditions that amount to cruel or inhuman treatment'.

[275] *Cf. e.g.* the Report of the mission to the United States of America on violence against women in state and federal prisons, UN Doc. E/CN.4/1999/68/Add.2, 1999, and the Report of the mission to Bangladesh, Nepal and India on the issue of trafficking of women and girls, with reference to the practice of 'protective custody' for victims of trafficking, UN Doc. E/CN.4/2001/73/Add.2, 6 February 2001.

[276] In its 2003 report the Special Rapporteur drew particular attention to the issue of criminalization of child victim of trafficking and sexual exploitation: 'Of particular concern is that children involved in prostitution or pornography are still being considered delinquents

ment of the highest attainable standard of physical and mental health,[277] the Special Rapporteur on the right to education,[278] the Special Rapporteur on the situation of human rights and fundamental freedoms of indigenous people,[279] and the Special Rapporteur on human rights of migrants.[280] Similarly, country-specific mechanisms, like the Special Rapporteur on the situation of human rights in the Palestinian territories occupied by Israel since 1967,[281] addressed the issue of deprivation of liberty of the child through their mandate.

63. The recent debate on responses to the threats of terrorism also has direct bearing on standards on protection in relation to deprivation of liberty. In 2004, the Office of the UN High Commissioner on Human Rights submitted a study on 'Protection of human rights and fundamental freedoms while countering terrorism',[282] indicating several developments of concern, not fully covered by the existing human rights mechanisms. Many of these issues are related to deprivation of liberty, including the principle of legality, detention at undisclosed locations, extraterritorial detention, restrictions to access to legal counsel and to habeas corpus proceedings.[283]

64. Apart from child rights and human rights law, other legal regimes of international law contain relevant standards on deprivation of liberty as well, often with direct relevance to the application of the CRC provisions. Refugee law, for instance, as based on the 1951 Convention relating to the Status of Refugees (and its 1967 Protocol) has been further elaborated in regard to children in the framework of

in certain countries and subject to judicial procedures'; he also raises the issue of 'protective custody' of children, UN Doc. *Cf.* E/CN.4/2003/79, 2003, paras.88 and 90.

[277] *Cf.* generally the report of the Special Rapporteur on the right to health, UN Doc.E/CN.4/2004/49, 2004.

[278] *Cf. e.g.* her report's reference to children in detention as likely to be excluded from access to education, UN Doc. E/CN.4/2003/9, 2003, para. 24.

[279] *Cf.* his report, UN Doc. E/CN.4/2004/80, 2004, with particular focus on aspects of discrimination and justice systems: 'Indigenous people tend to be over-represented in the criminal justice system, are often denied due process and are frequently victims of violence and physical abuse. Indigenous women and children are particularly vulnerable in this respect'.

[280] Her report contained in UN Doc. E/CN.4/2003/85, 2002, focussed on 'the human rights of migrants deprived of their liberty', including of children: 'According to the Special Rapporteur's information and personal observations, minors, including unaccompanied children, are at times detained for long or undetermined periods and deported under no clear authority and on discretional grounds, with no possibility of challenging the legality of the measure before a court or other competent, independent and impartial authority' (para. 47). She finally recommends States to ensure 'that the legislation does not allow for the detention of unaccompanied children' (Para. 75(a)).

[281] UN Doc. E/CN.4/2003/30, 2002, para. 38: 'Over 1,500 Palestinian children under the age of 18 have been arrested and detained since September 2000 in connection with crimes relating to the uprising. Most have been arrested on suspicion of throwing stones at Israeli soldiers'.

[282] UN Doc. A/59/428, 2004.

[283] *Ibid.,* para. 43.

the UN High Commissioner for Refugees' standard-setting activities.[284] Specific guarantees for children and specific standards on deprivation of liberty are also covered in the 1998 Guiding Principles on Internal Displacement.[285]

65. Finally, international humanitarian law addresses deprivation of liberty in relation to the responsibilities of the parties to international or non-international armed conflict. As civilians, for instance, they are provided protection through the 1949 Fourth Geneva Convention, and Article 77 ('Protection of Children') of the Additional Protocol I declares children to be 'the object of special respect and [they] shall be protected against any form of indecent assault.' Furthermore, they should not be recruited to armed forces and during any form of detention they should, in principle, be separated from adults. Articles 4 and 5 of the Additional Protocol II on non-international armed conflict contain further standards for the protection of children and persons deprived of their liberty.

66. Disrespect for these guarantees may result in the perpetrator's individual responsibility for genocide, crimes against humanity and war crimes, under international criminal law. In regard to deprivation of liberty of the child, the forcible transfer of children from one group of the population to another may fall under the jurisdiction of the International Criminal Court in relation to genocide (Article 6(e) of the 1998 Rome Statute);[286] moreover, 'enslavement; deportation or forcible transfer of population; imprisonment or other severe deprivation of physical liberty in violation of fundamental rules of international law; [. . .] enforced disappearance of persons' may all constitute crimes against humanity, 'when committed as part of a widespread or systematic attack directed against any civilian population, with knowledge of the attack (Article 7); and, *inter alia*, 'unlawful deportation or transfer or unlawful confinement' as well as the 'taking of hostages' may be considered war crimes under Article 8 of the Rome Statute.[287]

2. Regional Standards

67. Again on the regional level, all human rights treaties of a general nature contain provisions in regard to deprivation of liberty comparable, in principle, to Article 37(b), (c), (d) of the CRC, namely, the ECHR (Article 5), the 1969 American Convention on Human Rights (Articles 5, 7), the 1994 Arab Charter on Human Rights (Article 8), the 1981 African Charter on Human and Peoples' Rights (hereafter ACHPR) (Articles

---

[284] *Cf. e.g.* Refugee Children: Guidelines for Protection and Care, Chapter 7: Personal Liberty and Security UNHCR 1994; Guidelines on Policies and Procedures in Dealing with Unaccompanied Children Seeking Asylum, UNHCR 1997; *cf. infra* Part II, Chapter III 2.5.

[285] UN Doc. E/CN.4/1998/53/Add.2, 1998, Annex; *cf.*, in particular, to principles 4, 11 and 12.

[286] Rome Statute of the International Criminal Court (UN Doc. A/CONF.183/9) 17 July 1998.

[287] *Cf. e.g. International Criminal Justice and Children*, No Peace without Justice/UNICEF Innocenti Research Centre 2002.

5, 6) and—to a very limited extent—the African Charter on the Rights and Welfare of the Child (Article 17(2)(a)).

68. The ECHR differs in one important aspect from all other universal or regional treaties in relation to deprivation of liberty insofar, as it is the only document providing for an—exhaustive—list of grounds justifying interference with the right to personal liberty and security enshrined in the first sentence of Article 5(1).[288] This list includes grounds for permissible deprivation of liberty such as imprisonment after conviction or pre-trial detention, but also more controversial grounds like 'lawful detention [. . .] of persons of unsound mind, alcoholics or drug addicts or vagrants' or detention of children 'for the purpose of educational supervision'. The latter may include both measures under a child welfare and a juvenile justice regime, with strong emphasis on the stated aim, *i.e.* the intended educational effect.[289] Apart from that, the ECHR provides for a broad range of rights and safeguards for persons deprived of their liberty, including information rights, prompt hearing, trial within reasonable time, bail, habeas corpus proceedings and a right to compensation. There is no specific provision on human treatment during detention or imprisonment comparable to Article 37(c) of the CRC, compensated however by the general prohibition of torture, inhuman or degrading treatment or punishment. In this context, the 1987 European Convention for the Prevention of Torture and Inhuman or Degrading Treatment or Punishment[290] strives to prevent ill-treatment in places of detention through a visiting mechanism. The Council of Europe, furthermore, has adopted several policy recommendations on relevant criminal justice issues

---

[288] Article 5(1): 'Everyone has the right to liberty and security of person. No one shall be deprived of his liberty save in the following cases and in accordance with a procedure prescribed by law: (a) the lawful detention of a person after conviction by a competent court; (b) the lawful arrest or detention of a person for non-compliance with the lawful order of a court or in order to secure the fulfilment of any obligation prescribed by law; (c) the lawful arrest or detention of a person effected for the purpose of bringing him before the competent legal authority on reasonable suspicion of having committed an offence or when it is reasonably considered necessary to prevent his committing an offence or fleeing after having done so; (d) the detention of a minor by lawful order for the purpose of educational supervision or his lawful detention for the purpose of bringing him before the competent legal authority; (e) the lawful detention of persons for the prevention of the spreading of infectious diseases, of persons of unsound mind, alcoholics or drug addicts or vagrants; (f) the lawful arrest or detention of a person to prevent his effecting an unauthorised entry into the country or of a person against whom action is being taken with a view to deportation or extradition. The 4th Additional Protocol to the ECHR prohibits deprivation of liberty for debt (Article 1).

[289] *Cf.* the ECtHR case of *Bouamar v. Belgium,* 29 February 1988, *Publications of the Court,* Series A 129, para. 52; *cf.* also generally U. Kilkelly, *The child and the European Convention on Human Rights* (Aldershot, Ashgate Publications, 1999).

[290] *Cf.* U. Kriebaum, *Folterprävention in Europa—Die Europäische Konvention zur Verhütung von Folter und unmenschlicher oder erniedrigender Behandlung oder Bestrafung* (Vienna, Verlag Österreich, 2000).

here, most recently 'on new ways of dealing with juvenile delinquency and the role of juvenile justice'.[291]

69. Within the framework of the European Union, it should be noted that the 2000 EU Charter on fundamental rights and freedom only provides for the minimum guarantee of an explicit right to personal liberty and security (Article 6), taking into account, however, the complementary relationship to the ECHR standards (see Article 52(3)).

70. Under the Inter-American system, Article 7 of the ACHR offers a wide range of standards, based on the right to personal liberty and security and prohibiting any unlawful deprivation of one's 'physical' liberty, as well as 'arbitrary arrest or imprisonment'. Furthermore, information rights upon detention, prompt hearing and trial 'within a reasonable time', bail, habeas corpus and 'recourse to a court' even in case of a 'threat' of deprivation of liberty as well as prohibition of detention for debt are granted. Article 5 adds an explicit right to respect of the 'physical, mental and moral integrity' of the person and safeguards for human treatment during deprivation of liberty (including a separate prohibition of torture); accused persons shall be separated from convicted persons and children from adults.[292]

71. Compared to these standards, the African human rights regime is less comprehensive: Article 6 of the 1981 ACHPR provides for the right to liberty and security and the requirement of lawfulness of deprivation of liberty, 'in particular' prohibiting arbitrary arrest or detention. Article 7 continues with a right to a legal remedy and to trial within reasonable time. Thus, provisions on review of the legality of deprivation of liberty/habeas corpus are missing, and the African Charter does not contain specific rights for human treatment during deprivation of liberty, nor the basic requirements of separation of the various groups of detained persons (pre-trial—convicted, children—adults). The latter omission, however, is remedied by Article 17(2)(b) of the principal child-focussed African document, the 1990 African Charter on the Rights and Welfare of the Child, calling for strict separation of adults

---

[291] Committee of Ministers, *Recommendation (2003) 20*, of 24 September 2003.
[292] Already the 1948 (initially non-binding) American Declaration provides for a broad range of guarantees, including an explicit right to liberty and security of the person (Article 1), further elaborated by Article 25, which offers protection from unlawful (including *ex post facto* legislation) deprivation of liberty, from deprivation of liberty due to non-fulfilment of contractual obligations, the rights to habeas corpus, to a trial without undue delay, and to humane treatment during deprivation of liberty (in addition to the prohibition of torture and related treatment). Protection standards on deprivation of liberty are further complemented within the Inter-American system through various other instruments, such as the 1985 Inter-American Convention to Prevent and Punish Torture (without a system of preventive on-site visits, however), the 1989 Inter-American Convention on the International Return of Children and the 1994 Inter-American Convention on the Forced Disappearance of Persons and the 1994 Inter-American Convention on International Traffic in Minors.

from children (thereby with less flexibility than the CRC); besides, this Charter contains a double prohibition of torture, first on a general level (Article 16), second within the explicit context of deprivation of liberty (Article 17(2)(a)).[293]

[293] Interestingly, the African Charter on Welfare of the Child itself contains neither an express right to personal liberty and security nor a prohibition of unlawful or arbitrary deprivation of liberty of the child! *cf.*, more generally, on the Charter, Danwood Mzikenge Chirwa, 'The merits and demerits of the African Charter on the Rights and Welfare of the Child', *The International Journal of Children's Rights* 10, No. 2, 2002, pp. 157–177.

CHAPTER THREE

SCOPE OF ARTICLE 37(B), (C), (D)

1. Drafting History

72. The making of Article 37(b), (c), (d) resembles a test driving exercise. Starting from zero, it took the process quite some time to get into gear, with a remarkable twist at a cross-road only just before the finishing line. There were no provisions on deprivation of liberty in the very first 1978 proposal for the Draft Convention, and the first substantive discussions on deprivation of liberty started eight years later only in the 1986 Working Group, with growing numbers of (up to 15) paragraphs and sub-paragraphs in the draft article, of proposals submitted and intensity in the discussion. In December 1988, finally, a compromise working paper split the draft article into two separate provisions, one, *inter alia*, on deprivation of liberty (now Article 37) and another on juvenile justice (now Article 40), adopted in 1989 at last.

73. The first proposal for a Draft CRC, submitted by Poland in 1978, did not contain any provision on deprivation of liberty at all, simply because the 1959 Declaration on the Rights of the Child, which served as the rather literal model for the Polish initiative, did not address that matter. Only the revised Polish proposal of 1979, adopted then as the first basic working text by the newly set-up drafting Working Group of the Commission on Human Rights, provided for a very limited reference to deprivation of liberty, stating as an objective of penitentiary systems to 'enable the child to serve the sentence of deprivation or limitation of freedom in a special manner, and in particular, in separation from adult offenders'[294] (Para. 3 of then 'Article 20', the last in the list of substantive articles). The remainder of that article called for unspecific 'special treatment and privileges' of children in the penal system, prohibited capital punishment and called for punishments 'adequate to the particular phase of [the child's] development'.[295]

74. It took the drafting Working Group several years until its agenda touched again on these issues in the 1986 session. Poland and Canada, in particular, proposed much more elaborate draft articles now, encompassing a wide range of guarantees,

---

[294] Thus, making the principle of separation of children from adults in detention the 'oldest' of the various guarantees contained in the later Article 37.

[295] UN Doc. E/CN.4/1349, p. 6; for a reproduction of the *travaux préparatoires, cf.* S. Detrick, *o.c.* (note 252).

from due process and fair trial standards to torture prohibition and deprivation of liberty. Para. 1 of these proposals generally set the tone by referring to children within the penal system only, with objectives of juvenile justice as the over-all theme for the following paragraphs. Canada, which played an instrumental part during the whole process, provided a lengthy revised text which was based on provisions taken directly from the UDHR (Articles 9, 10, 11), the CCPR (Articles 6(5), 7, 9, 10 and 14) and the Beijing Rules (Rule 18 on alternative dispositions, Rule 19 on least possible use of institutionalisation, Rules 5 and 17 on the principle of proportionality of any reaction to juvenile offences).[296] No consensus could yet be achieved, partly because of the still unclear issue of how to best relate the CRC provisions to already existing human rights standards, and finally, an informal working party (Canada, Poland, Austria, International Commission of Jurists and other NGOs) prepared another revised proposal. Here, para. 2 took 'regard to the relevant provisions of other international instruments' and required States to ensure to the child '(a) as a minimum [. . .] in every appropriate aspect, the same legal rights as an adult accused or found guilty of infringing the penal law';[297] and it continues, by declaring '(b) Detention awaiting trial shall be used only as a measure of last resort, for the shortest possible period of time'.[298] Moreover, no child should be 'unnecessarily institutionalized' and the '[p]enal law and the penitentiary system shall not be used as a substitute for child welfare procedures and facilities'. Agreement was reached, however, only on the first paragraph of the draft article, recognizing the child's right in penal law proceedings to special child-adequate treatment. The rest of the article was subject to one more revision proposed by Canada, omitting the 'measure of last resort'-rule. In the ensuing discussion, as far as deprivation of liberty is concerned, consensus was reached on the inclusion of the following provision: '[n]o child is arbitrarily detained or imprisoned or subjected to torture, cruel, inhuman or degrading treatment or punishment'.[299] On the other hand, after a debate on an alternative wording for 'unnecessarily institutionalized', the latter was deleted altogether. The Netherlands asked for inclusion of the words 'according to the law' in relation to the child's right to maintain contact with the family, but withdrew in favour of 'save in exceptional circumstances'.[300] Regarding respect for the separation of children from adults, the United States sought to replace the qualifying phrase 'unless it is considered in the child's best interest not to do so' by the phrase 'or unless it has been determined appropriate that the child be treated as an adult'. This proposal rightly was rejected, with Algeria stating that by including such a provision, 'the purpose of the Convention would be defeated'.[301]

---

[296] UN Doc. E/CN.4/1986/39, para. 90.
[297] *Ibid.*, para. 93.
[298] *Cf.* Rule 13(1) of the 1985 Beijing Rules.
[299] UN Doc. E/CN.4/1986/39, para. 103.
[300] *Ibid.*, para. 122.
[301] *Ibid.*, para. 119.

75. As a result, the draft text adopted at the Working Group's first reading in 1988[302] contained provisions on deprivation of liberty within one very lengthy (then) Article 19, which dealt primarily with fair trial and criminal justice matters. This picture changed significantly in the following round of substantive considerations during the 1989 session of the Working Group. The UN Crime Prevention and Criminal Justice Branch submitted an extensive and challenging text on alternative approaches to children in conflict of the law and deprivation of liberty. It called for a general decriminalisation in regard to children and assistance to children 'to develop a sense of responsibility to assume a constructive role in society', for an abolition of status offences, *i.e.* behaviour not penalized if shown by adults, for diversion mechanisms and a separate juvenile justice system, and, most importantly in our context, it proposed States Parties to 'recognize that all forms of deprivation of liberty are detrimental to child growth and development. In principle, children should not be deprived of their liberty. Incarceration should always be a disposition of last resort and for the absolute minimum period necessary, with full protection of their rights and well-being'.[303] On the other hand, also Venezuela submitted a proposal introducing new provisions and wording as well as two additional draft articles on monitoring of children 'subjected to a measure restricting their liberty' and on protection of the child's privacy in relation to the press and other media.

76. In the following discussion 'it became obvious that there was a total lack of consensus',[304] and a broad drafting group[305] was asked for a compromise text. In the end, the informal drafting group came up with a completely new proposal,[306] splitting the existing draft article 19 now into two separate provisions (Article 19 and 19 *bis*), which are very close to today's provisions of Article 37 and Article 40. Members of that drafting group explained that they intended to prepare a 'text consistent with the instruments adopted in this field by the United Nations, dividing the various independent situations which required protection into two articles'.[307] Thus, the group on the one hand 'studied the deprivation of liberty, viewed so as to reflect the comments formulated by the Human Rights Committee[308] and

---

[302] UN Doc. E/CN.4/1988/WG.1/WP.1/Rev.2 (6 April 1988), pp. 23–25.

[303] UN Doc. E/CN.4/1989/WG.1/WP.2 (24 November 1988); *cf.* also UN Doc. E/CN.4/1989/48, para. 534.

[304] UN Doc. E/CN.4/1989/48, para. 536.

[305] Comprising of Argentina, Canada, China, Cuba, India, Mexico, Portugal, United States, USSR, Venezuela, later joined by other delegations and NGOs.

[306] UN Doc. E/CN.4/1989/WG.1/WP.67/Rev.1 (8 December 1988).

[307] It should be noted, however, that due to the separation of the articles the explicit reference 'to relevant provisions of international instruments' was kept with the new provision on juvenile justice only.

[308] In this context, the 1982 General Comments No. 8 on Article 9 of the CCPR (Right to liberty and security of persons, 1982 and No. 9 on Article 10 (Humane treatment of persons deprived of their liberty) are of particular relevance, *cf. Compilation of General Comments and General Recommendations adopted by Human Rights Treaty Bodies* (UN Doc. HRI/GEN/1/Rev.7, 12 May 2004). As far as the scope of application is concerned, for instance, General Comment

to show the respect due to human dignity, recognition of the needs of children and the concern to assure them legal or other assistance'; on the other hand, '[a]ware of the initiatives taken in the United Nations in the area of juvenile justice, the drafting group had incorporated some of the ideas in article 19*bis* [. . .]' (now Article 40).[309] By adopting such an approach, Article 37 got a much clearer profile, in particular as far as the provisions on deprivation of liberty are concerned. While lit. (b) contains safeguards in relation to the act of deprivation of liberty, lit. (c) focuses on safeguards during the state of deprivation of liberty, and lit. (d) establishes principles for review of such situations. Upon Argentina's suggestion, the new article 'would need some form of an introductory phrase', a *chapeau* to the article was inserted, requiring States Parties to 'ensure' the guarantees of Article 37.[310]

77. The proposal by the informal drafting group also showed remarkable terminological consistency in using the term 'deprivation of liberty' without exception (instead of 'arrest', 'detention', 'imprisonment' etc)—a feature lost, however, during the ensuing controversy in the plenary Working Group. The second paragraph of the new Article 19 initially read: 'No child shall be deprived of his or her liberty unlawfully or arbitrarily. Deprivation of liberty shall be used only as a measure of last resort and for the shortest possible period of time.' While there was rather quick consensus on the first sentence, the second proved more difficult to accept. According to the representative of Canada, who had introduced the text to the Working Group, the whole paragraph 'largely reflected both the International Covenant on Civil and Political Rights and the Beijing Rules'.[311] However, several delegates voiced concern about content taken from the latter, particularly as regards the reference to the 'shortest period of time'.[312] The representative of Germany opposed to it due to national legislation that 'does not insist that custodial sentences for juveniles should be "for the shortest possible period of time"'.[313] As a result the deletion of that phrase or even of the entire sentence was proposed; moreover, the USSR representative suggested 'that the broad notion of "deprivation of liberty" be replaced by the more precise words "imprisonment, arrest and detention" and that the text should indicate that the measures should be "in con-

---

No. 8 states: 'Article 9 which deals with the right to liberty and security of persons has often been somewhat narrowly understood in reports by States parties, and they have therefore given incomplete information. The Committee points out that paragraph 1 is applicable to all deprivations of liberty, whether in criminal cases or in other cases such as, for example, mental illness, vagrancy, drug addiction, educational purposes, immigration control, etc', *o.c.*, para. 1.

[309] UN Doc. E/CN.4/1989/48, para. 537.

[310] *Ibid.*, para. 538.

[311] *Ibid.*, para. 546.

[312] *Cf.* Rule 13.1. of the Beijing Rules, within the context of detention pending trial only, however.

[313] UN Doc. E/CN.4/1989/48, para. 549.

formity with the law"'.[314] The need for the latter was questioned by France, with reference to the principle of legality in the first sentence. Finally, the German delegate declared the need for the group to consult with criminal justice experts in the capitals before an agreement. Others stated, however, that proposals based on the Beijing Rules 'could not be necessarily considered as totally new'[315] while several delegate 'expressed their preference for a more specific language instead of a general reference such as "deprivation of liberty", since this term could also cover educational and other types of deprivation of liberty applied to minors besides detention, arrest, or imprisonment'.[316]

78. After all a compromise text was adopted, which retained principles taken from the Beijing Rules, but lost its consistent terminology: 'The arrest, detention or imprisonment of a child shall be in conformity with the law and shall be used only as a measure of last resort and for the shortest appropriate period of time'. The other paragraphs gave not rise for any more controversy at this stage: 'save in exceptional circumstances' was inserted to the right to maintain family contacts, and reference was made to the need to adopt a child's age and development orientation for conditions during deprivation of liberty (taken from Article 14(4) of the CCPR); finally, habeas corpus guarantees were amended as to 'correspond with relevant provisions of the International Covenant on Civil and Political Rights'.[317]

79. In brief, the drafting process of Art. 37(b), (c), (d) supports a commitment of the CRC to reduce deprivation of liberty of children as far as possible. It further reveals the clear need for attention to the specific requirements of children, including flexibility in the child's best interests (*e.g.* maintaining family contacts), in all such situations of deprivation of liberty; this emphasizes also the trend towards emancipation of deprivation of liberty standards from the narrower criminal law context to a broader scope of applicability. Certainly, this development benefited from parallel activities at that time in areas, such as juvenile justice (Beijing Rules, Riyadh Guidelines), institutionalisation and alternative measures (JDL Rules, Tokyo Rules). Still, several States had difficulties during the CRC drafting in accepting the new standards wholeheartedly for the CRC, as seen in the controversy about the second sentence of Article 37(b) (scope of application of 'last resort' principle). In this regard it was left to the UN JDL Rules adopted by the UN General Assembly (by consensus!) only one year after the CRC to explicitly state as a principle that 'deprivation of the liberty of a juvenile should be a disposition of last resort and for the minimum necessary period and should be limited to exceptional cases' (Rule 2).

---

[314] *Ibid.*, para. 551.
[315] *Ibid.*, para. 555.
[316] *Ibid.*, para. 556.
[317] *Ibid.*, para. 563; though, the reference there to 'court or other competent, independent and impartial authority' relates rather to Article 14(1) of the CCPR and not to the *habeas corpus* provision of Article 9(4).

2. Deprivation of Liberty of Children

2.1 Terms and Definitions

80. Before entering the discussion on deprivation of liberty standards it seems advisable to briefly discuss the term 'child', *i.e.* the holder of the rights enshrined in Article 37(b), (c), (d), first. This is because terminology in international law in relation to deprivation of liberty of children is not consistent in this respect.

81. The CRC defines the child as the bearer of its rights as any human person below the age of 18, with the exception of children reaching the age of majority earlier according to domestic law (Article 1)—the latter could already be seen as opening up a possible restriction of the application of Article 37 standards. And the relevant non-binding UN standards in this area use even different definitions: the Beijing Rules, while focusing on juvenile justice, speak of 'juveniles' without any age limit, but relate its scope to domestic legal systems dealing with 'an offence in a manner which is different from an adult' (Rule 2(2)), which would allow application to persons even above the age of 18 (*e.g.* for specific provisions on 'young adults'). The JDL Rules, on the other hand, plainly refer to a 'juvenile' as 'every person under the age of 18' (Rule 11(a)), without any restriction.

82. The reference to domestic law in Article 1 of the CRC must not be 'interpreted as a general escape clause, nor should it allow ages to be established which might be contrary to the principles and provisions of the Convention'[318] and, 'in general, minimum ages that are protective should be set as high as possible (for example protecting children from [. . .] custodial sentences)'.[319] With the over-all protective nature of standards on deprivation of liberty being evident,[320] it has to be concluded that the possible limitation in relation to the age of majority according to Article 1 of the CRC does not allow for a lowering of standards on deprivation of liberty. This is further confirmed by the Human Rights Committee monitoring CCPR implementation, which has stated in relation to deprivation of liberty and with reference to Article 6(5) of the CCPR that 'all persons under the age of 18 should be treated as juveniles, at least in matters relating to criminal justice'.[321] Moreover, it could well be argued that the JDL Rules have been adopted *after* the CRC, implying an international consensus towards exclusion of domestic restrictions on protec-

---

[318] OHCHR/UNITAR/UN Staff College Project, *Manual on Human Rights Reporting under Six Major International Human Rights Instruments* (Geneva, UN Publication, 1997), p. 415.
[319] R. Hodgkin and P. Newell, *Implementation Handbook for the Convention on the Rights of the Child* (second edition, New York—Geneva, UNICEF, 2002), p. 6.
[320] *Cf.* Rule 3 on the protective intention of the JDL Rules.
[321] Human Rights Committee, *General Comment No. 21 (1992) on humane treatment of persons deprived of their liberty (Article 10), o.c.* (note 308), para. 13.

tive age limits.[322] It follows from this that standards on deprivation of liberty in relation to children apply—in line with Rule 11(a) of the JDL Rules—to all children under the age of 18 as a minimum, without precluding higher age limits according to national standards, *e.g.* in the area of juvenile justice.

83. Another question concerns the setting of a specific minimum age for deprivation of liberty. While Article 40(3)(a) of the CRC only calls for the setting of an age of criminal responsibility, the CRC Committee in its Guidelines for periodic reports rightly distinguishes between those limits and asks States Parties specifically for information on the minimum legal age established by legislation on 'deprivation of liberty, including by arrest, detention and imprisonment, *inter alia* in the areas of administration of justice, asylum-seeking and placement of children in welfare and health institutions'.[323] In its State reporting practice the CRC Committee, however, is less precise and consistent, usually just referring to age limits of criminal responsibility, and showing seldom concern only specifically on the absence/too low of a minimum age for deprivation of liberty.[324] Still, the two age limits are certainly inter-linked in the area of criminal justice, because here, deprivation of liberty—be it arrest, pre-trial detention or imprisonment—will occur only as a response to a young person's behaviour, which will only be justified within the context of rules establishing criminal responsibility.[325] Consequently, the Committee's discussion of the age of criminal responsibility gives a strong indication towards a minimum age for deprivation of liberty acceptable under the CRC in relation to juvenile justice.[326] Following this argument, the Committee may regard age limits below the age of 12 or even 14 as too low an acceptable standard for deprivation of liberty here.[327]

---

[322] J.W. Tobin, Time to remove the shackles: The legality of restraints on children deprived of their liberty under international law, *The International Journal of Children's Rights* 9, 2001, p. 216.

[323] CRC Committee, *General Guidelines regarding the form and the contents of the periodic reports* (UN Doc. CRC/C/58, 1996), para. 24.

[324] *Cf.* CRC Committee, *Concluding Observations: Panama* (UN Doc. CRC/C/15/Add.68, 1997) para. 21: 'the apparent absence in national legislation of minimum ages below which a child may not be deprived of liberty [...] causes deep concern to the Committee'. *Cf.* also here with reference to Articles 10(2) and 24 of the CCPR, the Human Rights Committee's 'profound concern that children, including children under 10 years of age, are held in detention on remand', *Concluding Observations: Guyana* (UN Doc. CCPR/C/79/Add.121, 2000), para. 16.

[325] For an overview on the age of criminal responsibility, *cf.* UNICEF, *Juvenile Justice, Innocenti Digest N. 3* (Florence, UNICEF, 1998).

[326] *Cf.* also G. Van Bueren, *o.c.* (note 239), p. 208, concluding that, 'it is implicit in the Convention that any minimum age established by national law relating to criminal capacity will also be the same minimum age below which children could not be deprived of their liberty for breaches of the penal law'. Apart from that this should not distract from the overall relevance of the CRC principle of using deprivation of liberty only as 'measure of last resort', *cf. infra* Part II, Chapter III/2.5.

[327] For instance, the CRC Committee welcomed Morocco's new Penal Procedure Code, giving special protection to all children in conflict with the law from 12 to 18 years: CRC

84. After considering the notions of 'child' and 'juvenile' it is now time to discuss in more detail the term 'deprivation of liberty' itself. For a start, still, one has to note that any discussion thereto should take into account two underlying and inter-linked considerations: first, examination of standards on deprivation of liberty usu-ally tends to focus on the 'negative side', the limitation of a human right, the compliance with laws and formal procedures. The ensuing challenge, thus, lies in not losing sight of the right to be protected here, namely personal liberty of the child: the implications for a young person of not being able to move around freely and leave places at will are both evident and far-reaching, considering, not least, the State Party's obligation to ensure the child's most conducive personal devel-opment as a general principle of the CRC (Article 6(2)).

85. As a consequence, interferences into personal liberty as a fundamental aspect of the child's development should be limited to the absolute minimum, with the ultimate goal of avoiding deprivation of liberty. This is the essence of the various international UN standards developed in the 1980s and 1990s, stressing the need for specific treatment of children.[328] Another argument for avoidance of depriva-tion of liberty relates to the danger of 'criminal contamination' when submitted to the criminal justice system[329] and the specific dependency and vulnerability of chil-dren 'to abuse, victimization and the violation of their rights'.[330] Thus, any intended restriction of personal liberty must pass a specific impact assessment with a view to minimizing harm to the child's development and maximizing respect for his or her rights; particular attention should be paid in this regard to the stated purpose of deprivation of liberty (*e.g.* punishment, public security, the child's personal secu-rity) and its proper justification.[331]

Committee, *Concluding Observations: Morocco* (UN Doc. CRC/C/15/Add.211, 2003), para. 66; yet, and more specifically in relation to deprivation of liberty, the Committee stated vis-à-vis the United Kingdom, it is 'particularly concerned that since the State party's initial report, children between 12 and 14 years of age are now being deprived of their liberty'. It further continues, '[m]ore generally, the Committee is deeply concerned at the increasing number of children who are being detained in custody at earlier ages for lesser offences and for longer sentences imposed as a result of the recently increased court powers to issue deten-tion and restraining orders': CRC Committee, *Concluding Observations: United Kingdom* (UN Doc. CRC/C/15/Add.188, 2002), para. 59.

[328] *Cf.* Rule 2 of the JDL Rules for general guidance, Rule 17 on pre-trial detention, Rule 13.1 and 17.1(b) of the Beijing Rules; G. Van Bueren, *o.c.* (note 239), p. 206: 'International law has not yet reached the stage where states are prepared to accept an absolute prohibition on the imprisonment of children. There is, however, a perceptible trend moving in this direction'.

[329] Commentaries to Rules 1 (Fundamental perspectives), 8 (Protection of privacy), 11 (Diversion), 13 (Detention pending trial), 19 (Least possible use of institutionalisation) of the Beijing Rules.

[330] Preamble to the JDL Rules, relevant to all other situations of deprivation of liberty beyond detention as well.

[331] *Cf.*, for instance, Article 5(1)(d) of the ECHR which provides for deprivation of liberty for 'educational purposes'; the ECtHR in the case of *Bouamar v. Belgium*, 29 February 1988,

86. It should be noted here that while being included in most of the universal and regional human rights treaties,[332] the right to personal liberty is not expressly repeated in the CRC, which is more concerned with safeguards for its limitation in Article 37(b), (c), (d). Nevertheless, this fundamental right is guaranteed to every person, including children, by Article 3 of the 1948 UDHR already; moreover, conceptually, protection of the right to personal liberty is inherent to standards concerning deprivation of liberty—*e contrario* disregard for those standards leads to a violation of the human right to personal liberty.[333] As far as the notion 'liberty' is concerned, this should not be confused with concepts of human freedom; instead, personal liberty relates to freedom of bodily movement in the narrowest sense.[334] As Nowak notes, '[a]n interference with personal liberty results only from the forceful detention of a person at a certain, narrowly bounded location', citing a broad range of examples, such as: prisons or other detention facilities, psychiatric institutions, facilities for re-education, work camps, facilities for treatment of drug addicts 'as well as an order of house arrest'.[335] This excludes, on the other hand, less restrictive limits on movement, like 'limitations on domicile or residency, exile, confinement to an island or expulsion from State territory',[336] which fall under the scope of the right to freedom of movement.[337]

87. As mentioned earlier, the CRC focuses on the 'negative side' of personal liberty by providing for standards on deprivation of liberty in Article 37, both in regard to the act of deprivation and to conditions and treatment during deprivation. And all of the provisions in lit. (b), (c) and (d) use the term 'deprivation of liberty'— with one notable exception in Article 37(b), where reference is made explicitly to 'arrest, detention or imprisonment'. As there is no definition of 'deprivation of liberty' provided in the CRC, thus, the question of its scope of application arises. The

---

Series A, No. 129, applied a strict standard, finding a violation of the right to personal liberty of a 17-year old boy who was repeatedly placed in a remand prison due to lack of adequate institutions for educational supervision.

[332] *Cf. supra* Part II, chapter II for further discussion.

[333] On the relationship between the right and its limitation, *cf.* M. Nowak, *o.c.* (note 255), Article 9, para. 2: '[The human right to personal liberty] obligates a State's legislature to define precisely the cases in which deprivation of liberty is permissible and the procedures to be applied and to make it possible for the independent judiciary to take quick action in the event of arbitrary or unlawful deprivation of liberty by administrative authorities or executive officials'.

[334] *Ibid.*, para. 3.

[335] *Ibid.*, para. 3, with further examples of the Human Rights Committee's case law under the individual complaint procedure.

[336] *Ibid.*, para. 3. *Cf.*, however, in regard to cumulation of factors leading to deprivation of liberty the ECtHR case of *Guzzardi v. Italy*, 6 November 1980, Series A, No. 39, para. 95.

[337] Articles 12 and 13 of the CCPR, *cf.* Human Rights Committee, *General Comment No 27 (1999): Freedom of movement (Article 12)*, *o.c.* (note 308). The CRC does not contain a similar provision; such a discussion will raise issues in relation to parental rights on determining residence and stay of their child as well as legislation on youth protection.

Human Rights Committee, already in its 1982 General Comment No 8 on the CRC's equivalent provision of Article 9(1) CCPR, states that this provision 'is applicable to all deprivations of liberty, whether in criminal cases or in other cases such as, for example, mental illness, vagrancy, drug addiction, educational purposes, immigration control, etc.'[338] The most pertinent international UN document in this regard has been adopted by the UN General Assembly one year after the CRC: the UN Rules for the Protection of Juveniles Deprived of their Liberty.[339] Rule 11(b) now offers a similarly broad definition to deprivation of liberty, as 'any form of detention or imprisonment or the placement of a person in a public or private custodial setting, from which this person is not permitted to leave at will, by order of any judicial, administrative or other public authority'. In short, deprivation of liberty here is relevant in all instances of a child being confined to a certain limited area without permission to leave at will by order of a State authority.[340] This includes typical cases of arrest, detention and imprisonment[341] and the juvenile justice context at large, but also includes situations of child refugees in administrative detention pending deportation,[342] and, moreover, extends further to the placement of children in closed institutions, like mentally handicapped children held in custodial settings.[343]

88. The CRC Committee in its 1996 Guidelines for Periodic Reports—under the heading of 'Children deprived of their liberty, including any form of detention, imprisonment or placement in custodial settings'—expressly refers to this JDL definition for its request of information on the State Party's implementation of Article 37(b).[344] And the Committee's practice under the State reporting mechanism, in principle,

---

[338] Human Rights Committee, *General Comment No. 8 (1982): Right to liberty and security of persons (Article 9)*, para. 1, *o.c.* (note 308). The drafters of the CRC provision at the 1989 Working group explicitly referred to the Human Rights Committee's practice in preparing the draft text, *cf. supra* chapter III/1.

[339] General Assembly Resolution 45/133 (14 December 1990), annex.

[340] UNICEF, in a recent publication, uses the following definition: 'Deprivation of liberty refers to placement of a child in any kind of establishment from which he or she cannot leave at will', UNICEF, *Justice for Children: Detention as a last Resort—Innovative Initiatives in the East Asia and Pacific Region* (Bangkok, UNICEF, 2004), p. 6.

[341] According to the 1988 Body of Principles for the Protection of All Persons under Any Form of Detention or Imprisonment (GA Res. 43/173, 9 December 1988), 'arrest' is defined as 'the act of apprehending a person for the alleged commission of an offence or by the action of an authority', whereas 'detention' and 'imprisonment' relate to 'the condition' of a person deprived of personal liberty, depending whether or not following a conviction for an offence.

[342] *Cf.* also the clarified mandate of the UN Working Group on Arbitrary Detention, *supra* Part II, Chapter II/2.

[343] *Cf.* also CRC Committee, *Day of General Discussion on the Administration of Juvenile Justice* (13th *November 1995*) (UN Doc. CRC/C/43, 1995), paras. 228–229.

[344] CRC Committee, *General Guidelines for periodic reports*, *o.c.* (note 323), para. 138; *cf.* also G. Van Bueren, *o.c.* (note 239), p. 211: 'The Committee ought to use the Rules for the Protection of Juveniles Deprived of their Liberty as a normative framework'.

confirms this broad interpretation of the scope of deprivation of liberty, although the Committee has a tendency to use at times rather generic terms and recommendations,[345] with still a strong leaning towards the juvenile justice context.

89. Nevertheless, a closer examination of the Committee's practice shows a wide range of cases falling under the scope of deprivation of liberty: for instance, the Committee has expressed its concern about arbitrary arrest and detention of street children,[346] arrest and detention of children accused of prostitution, 'vagrancy' or 'uncontrollable behaviour',[347] detention in police cells for up to several months,[348] prolonged detention in police custody due to lack of juvenile detention facilities,[349] 'preventive detention' of children,[350] 'protective custody' for children under the age of 12,[351] police custody for children accused of terrorism,[352] frequent recourse to pre-trial detention,[353] provisions allowing for mentally ill children to be detained,[354] detention of children 'beyond parental control' and detention of children 'at her Majesty's pleasure',[355] sentencing children 'at the President's pleasure',[356] long periods of imprisonment of children,[357] children detained in 'corrective labour institutions',[358] placement of children in 'centres for temporary isolation, adaptation and

[345] *Cf. e.g.* CRC Committee, *Concluding Observations: Germany* (UN Doc. CRC/C/15/Add.226, 2004), para. 61(b): 'Ensure that deprivation of liberty is only used as a measure of last resort, for the shortest possible time, that guarantees of due process are fully respected and that persons under 18 are not detained with adults'. For a critical assessment of the Committee's statements in relation to juvenile justice, *cf.* B. Abramson, *o.c.* (note 247).

[346] CRC Committee, *Concluding Observations: Indonesia* (UN Doc. CRC/C/15/Add.223, 2004), paras. 76, 80.

[347] CRC Committee, *Concluding Observations: Bangladesh* (UN Doc. CRC/C/15/Add.74, 1997), para. 26.

[348] CRC Committee, *Concluding Observations: New Zealand* (UN Doc. CRC/C/15/Add.216, 2003), para. 49. *Cf.* also, *Jamaica* (UN Doc. CRC/C/15/Add.32/1995), para. 17.

[349] CRC Committee, *Concluding Observations: St. Vincent and the Grenadines* (UN Doc. CRC/C/15/Add.184, 2002), para. 52(e).

[350] CRC Committee, *Concluding Observations: Panama* (UN Doc. CRC/C/15/Add.233, 2004), para. 60.

[351] CRC Committee, *Concluding Observations: Czech Republic* (UN Doc. CRC/C/15/Add.201, 2003), para. 66(b).

[352] CRC Committee, *Concluding Observations: Spain* (UN Doc. CRC/C/15/Add.185, 2002), paras. 53, 54.

[353] CRC Committee, *Concluding Observations: Madagascar* (UN Doc. CRC/C/15/Add.218, 2003), paras. 67-69.

[354] CRC Committee, *Concluding Observations: Nepal* (UN Doc. CRC/C/15/Add.57, 1996), para. 24.

[355] CRC Committee, *Concluding Observations: Nigeria* (UN Doc. CRC/C/15/Add.61, 1996), para. 21.

[356] CRC Committee, *Concluding Observations: Zambia* (UN Doc. CRC/C/15/Add.206, 2003), paras. 70, 72(a).

[357] CRC Committee, *Concluding Observations: Viet Nam* (UN Doc. Doc. CRC/C/15/Add.3, 1993), para. 6.

[358] CRC Committee, *Concluding Observations: Azerbaijan* (UN Doc. CRC/C/15/Add.77, 1997), para. 49.

rehabilitation',[359] 'secure training orders' for children aged 12 to 14,[360] (unaccompanied) child asylum-seekers held in detention centres,[361] placement of children for status offences,[362] children 'serving custodial sentences in social care institutions',[363] detention of juvenile offenders with 'children institutionalized for behavioural problems,[364] or parental authority allowing placement of children in prison ('*correction paternelle*').[365]

90. The last example refers to a situation actually not covered by the JDL definition, namely interferences with personal liberty through private actors (*i.e.* without state order). Examples include the abduction and detention of children by criminal organisations for trafficking or blackmail or enforced disappearances by rebel groups in conflict areas for terrorizing relatives etc are usually not discussed within the context of Article 37 of the CRC as a human rights/deprivation of liberty issue. Still, it has to be regarded as one important aspect of the State Party's obligation to protect children from interference with their rights.[366]

91. This leads to the still unresolved issue of State obligations vis-à-vis parental responsibilities in regard to deprivation of liberty of their children. The CRC Committee in 2003 criticized Haiti for its legislation on '*correction paternelle*', allowing parents under their parental authority to place their child in prison for up to six months 'without involvement of a court or a similar body'. Interestingly, the Committee while recommending the over-all abolishment of these legal provisions, found a violation of Article 37(d) here only (not: (b)!).[367] On the European level, in the controversial *Nielsen v. Denmark* case the ECtHR in 1988 held (by a small majority of 9–7) that the hospitalisation of a 12-year old boy against his will in a psychiatric ward of a State hospital, at the request of his mother (as holder of sole custody over the child) but without medical indication (against the background of a longstanding custody dispute between the parents), for more than five months did not

---

[359] CRC Committee, *Concluding Observations: Kazakhstan* (UN Doc. CRC/C/15/Add.213, 2003), para. 66.

[360] CRC Committee, *Concluding Observations: United Kingdom* (UN Doc. CRC/C/15/Add.34, 1995), para. 18.

[361] CRC Committee, *Concluding Observations: Austria* (UN Doc. CRC/C/15/Add.98, 1999), para. 27; Australia (UN Doc. CRC/C/15/Add.79, 1997), para. 20; *Canada* (UN Doc. CRC/C/15/Add.37, 1995), para. 24.

[362] CRC Committee, *Concluding Observations: Libya* (UN Doc. CRC/C/15/Add.209, 2003), para. 45(b).

[363] CRC Committee, *Concluding Observations: Egypt* (UN Doc. CRC/C/15/Add.5, 1993), para. 8.

[364] CRC Committee, *Concluding Observations: The Netherlands* (UN Doc. CRC/C/15/Add.227, 2004), para. 58(c).

[365] CRC Committee, *Concluding Observations: Haiti* (UN Doc. CRC/C/15/Add.202, 2003), paras. 28, 29.

[366] *Cf. infra* Part II, Chapter III/2.2.2.

[367] CRC Committee, *Concluding Observations: Haiti* (UN Doc. CRC/C/15/Add.202, 2003), paras. 28, 29.

constitute deprivation of liberty within the meaning of Article 5(1) of the ECHR, but should be seen as 'a responsible exercise by his mother of her custodial rights in the interest of the child' and thereby rejected State responsibility.[368] As Van Bueren notes, that judgement 'leaves children deprived of their liberty on the wishes of one or both parents, but against their own wishes, wholly unprotected'.[369] Parental rights are not unlimited, but subject to review also under the State obligation to protect the child from interferences by the parents.[370] Even cases of restriction of liberty within the family context (*e.g.* as a disciplinary measure) should fall under the scope of safeguards for deprivation of liberty, including the prohibition of arbitrariness and the principle of last resort.[371]

2.2   State Obligations in General

92. Under Article 2(1) of the CRC States Parties are obliged to 'respect and ensure' all CRC rights to all children under their jurisdiction. The Human Rights Committee, in discussing the comparable[372] provision of Article 2(1) of the CCPR further explains that, this legal obligation 'is both negative and positive in nature',[373] requiring restraint of the government in relation to interferences with human rights (*e.g.* no arbitrary arrest of street children) on the one hand and the adoption of comprehensive measures to fulfil their obligations (*e.g.* provide for adequate training of law enforcement personnel) on the other hand. The fundamental obligation to implement CRC rights contained in Article 4 of the CRC requires States Parties to undertake 'all appropriate legislative, administrative, and other measures'[374] and, more specifically, Article 37 calls on States Parties to 'ensure' all of its following guarantees, reminding them, in particular, of their positive obligations towards realization of the rights provided for by this article. This reminder is of particular importance for issues of deprivation of liberty, because for much too long, discussion here has centred around the question of State's non-interference with personal liberty and observance of procedural safeguards only. The positive obligation

---

[368] ECtHR, *Nielsen v. Denmark*, 28 November 1988, Series A, No. 144, para. 73.

[369] G. Van Bueren, *o.c.* (note 239), p. 213.

[370] 'International law is therefore establishing boundaries within which states are under a duty to ensure that parental power is properly exercised and within limits', G. Van Bueren, *o.c.* (note 239), p. 73. *Cf.* also CRC Committee, *Day of General Discussion on the Role of the Family in the Promotion of the Rights of the Child (10ᵗʰ October 1994)* (UN Doc. CRC/C/24, 1994), para. 197: 'The Convention is, furthermore, the most appropriate framework in which to consider, and to ensure respect for, the fundamental rights of all family members, in their individuality'.

[371] This raises questions also about appropriate educational measures (in line with Article 5 of the CRC), and issues relating to areas such as protection from all forms of violence and maltreatment as well as inhuman or degrading treatment or punishment of children.

[372] *Cf.* S. Detrick, *o.c.* (note 253), p. 68.

[373] Human Rights Committee, *General Comment No. 31 (2004): The Nature of the General Legal Obligation Imposed on States Parties to the Covenant*, *o.c.* (note 308), p. 192 *et seq.*

[374] *Cf.* CRC Committee, *General Comment No. 5 (2003) on General measures of implementation of the Convention on the Rights of the Child*, *o.c.* (note 308), p. 332 *et seq.*

to ensure, however, goes far beyond; it encompasses not just provisional duties of
the State Party to offer certain services and structures, like educational measures
for children deprived of their liberty, but also protection duties for children from
interferences by private actors, in the context of enforced disappearances, for
instance. Hence, States Parties signed up for a broad range of obligations to be
ensured under Article 37(b), (c), (d), and the principle extent of their implementation duties will be further examined in the following paragraphs. For a general
picture, it could be stated that Article 37(b) bears relevance especially for obligations to respect and to protect personal liberty of the child, while Article 37(c) and
(d) emphasize State obligations to fulfil those standards through comprehensive
positive action.

2.2.1   Obligation to Respect

93. The obligation to respect the right of the child to personal liberty, as guaranteed already by the UDHR and the CCPR, requires States Parties to refrain from any
interference without proper justification provided for by international and national
law. Article 37(b) of the CRC demands that deprivation of liberty as an interference
to this liberty must satisfy certain criteria, such as lawfulness and non-arbitrariness, and pass specific tests, like qualifying as a measure of last resort and for the
shortest appropriate period of time, in order to receive justification. If not, legiti-
macy of the interference is lost, and the child's right to personal liberty is violated.
In particular, the aspect of arbitrariness of interventions is of relevance here, which
goes beyond formal compliance with legal provisions by adding 'elements of injus-
tice, unpredictability, unreasonableness, capriciousness and unproportionality'.[375]
Because of this fundamental importance, the Human Rights Committee declared
that arbitrary deprivations of liberty may not be justified not even during public
emergencies (by invoking Article 4 of the CCPR).[376]

94. Privatisation of services and of other formally State-run activities, like administration of refugee detention facilities or prisons, does not take away State responsibilities for protection of personal liberty. Due to lower levels of direct involvement
of the State, however, the focus may shift, from obligations to respect to obligations to protect and fulfil, *e.g.* by establishing mechanisms for supervision and monitoring. The CRC Committee concluded in 2002 that 'the State continues to be bound
by its obligations under the treaty, even when the provision of services is dele-
gated to non-State actors', and that this 'includes the obligation to ensure that non-
State service providers operate in accordance with its provisions'. With reference
to Article 3(3) of the CRC, the Committee states that it 'establishes the obligation

---

[375] M. Nowak, *o.c.* (note 255), Article 9, para. 29.
[376] Human Rights Committee, *General Comment No. 29 (2001): States of Emergency (Article 4)*,
o.c. (note 308), para. 11.

of the State party to set standards in conformity with the Convention and ensure compliance by appropriate monitoring of institutions, services and facilities including of a private nature'.[377]

95. Obligations to respect have to be uphold also in light of recent anti-terrorism legislation and practice; after examining India's State Party report, for instance, the CRC Committee remained 'deeply concerned' by the use of the 2002 Prevention of Terrorism Act for the prosecution of children by special courts.[378] Earlier, it recommended to Peru that a Decree be 'repealed or amended', which provided liability of children suspected of being involved in terrorist activities, in order to bring it in line with respect for Article 37.[379] The Committee also strongly criticized specific legislation in El Salvador targeting children as part of a 'Tough Hand Plan' and 'Anti-Gang Laws', leading also to large numbers of children in detention.[380]

2.2.2   Obligation to Protect

96. Related to the obligation of the State not to interfere with personal liberty of the child is the State obligation to protect the child from interference through private actors. From the child's point of view, it is of less concern whether it has been locked up in a room by State police or rebel groups or agents of a child trafficking network or even its own parents.[381] Therefore, the issue at stake for the State Party is not to refrain from intervention, but to the contrary, to take positive action[382] to avoid the restriction of personal liberty through private persons, thus, acknowledging horizontal effects of the child's right to personal liberty. Most commonly, domestic legislation in criminal law, civil law or youth welfare law aims to protect the child's personal liberty in this regard.

97. Yet the scope of such horizontal effects of the child's personal liberty is still widely unexplored. In relation to personal security, the Human Rights Committee has found violations of that right under the CCPR through harassment and

---

[377] Recommendations of the Day of General Discussion: *The Private Sector as Service Provider and its Role in Implementing Child Rights (20 September 2002)* (UN Doc. CRC/C/121, 2002), paras. 1, 3.

[378] CRC Committee, *Concluding Observations: India* (UN Doc. CRC/C/15/Add.228, 2004), para. 78. *Cf.* also the Committee's concern on the impact of recent legislation in Spain on children accused of terrorism, UN Doc. CRC/C/15/Add.185, 2002, para. 53.

[379] CRC Committee, *Concluding Observations: Peru* (UN Doc. CRC/C/15/Add.8, 1993), para. 18.

[380] CRC Committee, *Concluding Observations: El Salvador* (UN Doc. CRC/C/15/Add.232, 2004), para. 67.

[381] Deprivation of the child's liberty here is often closely linked to illicit acts across national borders, requiring inter-state cooperation; increasingly this is governed by international treaties apart from human rights conventions, in areas such as organized crime and prevention of trafficking of children, international adoption, abduction of children by their parents *etc.* (*cf. supra* Part II, Chapter II).

[382] *Cf.* M. Nowak, *Introduction to the International Human Rights Regime* (Leiden—Boston, Martinus Nijhoff Publishers, 2003), p. 50 *et seq.*

intimidation of a person, or death threats and assassination attempts.[383] As far as the freedom of movement under Article 12 of the CCPR is concerned, the Human Rights Committee has acknowledged State Parties' obligations to protect individuals 'not only from public but also from private interference', declaring incompatible with Article 12 of the CCPR any law or practice that would, for example, require a women's decision on her place of residence to be subject to another third person's consent (*e.g.* a relative/husband).[384] Within the context of prevention of violence and State obligations under Article 19 of the CRC, the CRC Committee explicitly called for a 'review [of] all relevant legislation to ensure that all forms of violence against children, however light, are prohibited, [. . .] for punishment or disciplining within the child justice system, or in any other context',[385] and referred to the need to provide 'appropriate assistance to the parents and legal guardians in their child-rearing responsibilities, which includes addressing all forms of family violence'.[386] Unfortunately, the CRC Committee has not yet addressed the question of protection of personal liberty of the child within the family context in similar clear words.[387] In the end, the issue of horizontal effects of the child's personal liberty becomes pertinent in relation to all types of locations where children are held against their will.

2.2.3   *Obligation to Fulfil*

98. The obligation to fulfil requires States Parties to realize the child's personal liberty and safeguards on deprivation of liberty through comprehensive positive action. The CRC Committee in its 2003 General Comment on General Measures of Implementation[388] calls for the 'development of a children's rights perspective throughout Government, parliament, and the judiciary', which 'is required for effective implementation of the whole Convention.' It then offers a principal check-list of relevant activities to undertake, including: withdrawal of reservations to CRC provisions; ratification of other key human rights treaties; review of legislation; provision of effective remedies; a comprehensive rights-based national strategy; coordination mechanisms; mechanisms for CRC compliance in decentralized/federal States; safeguards for compliance after privatisation of services; child impact

---

[383] *Cf.* M. Nowak, *o.c.* (note 255), Article 9, para. 9, with references to case-law of the Human Rights Committee.

[384] Human Rights Committee, *General comment No. 27 (1999): Article 12 (Freedom of movement)*, *o.c.* (note 308), para. 6.

[385] CRC Committee, *Day of General Discussion on State violence children (22 September 2000)* (UN Doc. CRC/C/97, 1997), para. 688(8).

[386] CRC Committee, *Day of General Discussion on violence against children, within the family and in schools (28th September 2001)* (UN Doc. CRC/C/111, 2001), para. 725 *et seq.* on the issue of horizontal effects.

[387] *Cf.* also, G. Van Bueren, *o.c.* (note 239), p. 227.

[388] CRC Committee, *General Comment No. 5 (2003) General measures of implementation for the Convention on the Rights of the Child, o.c.* (note 308), p. 332 *et seq.*

assessment, evaluation and other monitoring activities; disaggregated data collection and research; budgetary allocations; training, child rights education and awareness-raising; establishment of independent human rights (ombuds)institutions; cooperation with civil society; cooperation with children directly; and international cooperation.

99. The Committee practice shows that all of these areas of implementation have direct relevance for the protection of standards on deprivation of liberty: several States Parties have declared reservations upon signature or ratification of the CRC in relation to Article 37, especially to Article 37(c), concerning separation of children from adults during deprivation of liberty. The CRC Committee consistently calls for a withdrawal of these reservations, and signalled particular concern in regard to non-separation of children, when 'it appears that only resource considerations now prevent the withdrawal of the reservation'.[389] As far as implementation of other relevant international standards is concerned, the Committee regularly refers (as a minimum) to the Beijing Rules, the Riyadh Guidelines, the JDL Rules, and the 1997 (Vienna) Guidelines for Action on Children in the Criminal Justice System. Here, however, also lies a weakness in the Committee's practice so far, as it deals with deprivation of liberty almost exclusively in a juvenile justice setting, but not that comprehensively as foreseen by its own definition based on the JDL Rules, which includes any form of placement in closed settings.[390] Thus, a rather frequent recommendation to States Parties addresses the need for a 'comprehensive review' of existing legislation and practice, based on a 'holistic approach',[391] but directed mostly to the establishment of a juvenile justice system only[392] and including typically a rather generic recommendation on deprivation of liberty as

---

[389] CRC Committee, *Concluding Observations: United Kingdom* (UN Doc. CRC/C/15/Add.188, 2002), paras. 6 and 7. Other States Parties having adopted reservations to Article 37 with relevance to deprivation of liberty include: Australia (separation of children from adults); Myanmar (prevalence of domestic law; withdrawn 1993); Canada (separation of children from adults); Cook Islands (separation of children from adults); Iceland ("Declaration"—separation of children from adults); Japan (separation mandatory below age of 20); Netherlands (including Antilles and Aruba—adult penal law applicable for juveniles aged 16 or older; separation of children from adults); Switzerland (separation of children from adults); New Zealand (separation of children from adults); Singapore (domestic law prevails—objections to reservation from Belgium, Norway).

[390] In its concluding observations, standards on deprivation of liberty are usually discussed under the 'special protection measures', sub-section on juvenile justice. Only exceptionally, reference is made to Article 37 in sections on 'family environment and alternative care' or education, as in the case of the United Kingdom: CRC Committee, *Concluding Observations: the United Kingdom* (UN Doc. CRC/C/15/Add.188), 2002, paras. 40, 47 and 48.

[391] Cf., e.g., CRC Committee, *Concluding Observations: Belgium* (UN Doc. CRC/C/15/Add.178, 2002), para. 31.

[392] B. Abramson uses the comparably high number of Committee calls for comprehensive review (app. one out of seven states) as an indicator for the over-all neglect of juvenile justice standards by States Parties, including avoidance of detention, B. Abramson, *o.c.* (note 247), I/1.

a measure of last resort and for the shortest appropriate period of time. Only seldomly the Committee devotes at least a separate sub-paragraph to issues of detention etc.[393]

100. The State obligation to fulfil Article 37 standards through provision of training to professionals (*e.g.* in the field of law enforcement, the judiciary, but also in child and youth welfare administration, social work etc.), is another area lacking a distinct focus of the CRC Committee in its concluding observations. More principally, in the course of the 2000 Discussion Day on State violence the Committee nevertheless called for standard-setting for professional qualification of all persons 'working in institutions caring for children, in alternative systems, in the police, and in juvenile penal institutions, including the condition that they not have a prior record of violence'. Furthermore, child rights training is asked for all those professionals, including content such as non-violent methods of discipline (together with anti-bullying and anti-violence strategies and policies), alternatives to institutionalisation, and child development. In addition, 'schemes for judges and magistrates to work with probation and social work staff to assess non-custodial alternatives' should be introduced.[394] However, these recommendations are usually not taken up in the Committee's consideration of State Party reports. In almost all discussions on juvenile justice, recommendations for training are included, but only exceptionally,[395] explicit reference is made to training related to the specific circumstances of children deprived of their liberty and capacity building for professionals in various forms of closed institutions and custodial settings, as required by Rule 85 *et seq.* of the JDL Rules.

101. The collection of relevant data, statistics and research as a precondition for policy formulation and priority setting constitutes a recurrent important issue in CRC Committee considerations. After its General Discussion Day on State Violence, the Committee recommended that '[a]ccurate, up-to-date and disaggregated data should be collected on the numbers and condition of children living in institutions or in the care of the State, held in pre-trial detention or in police stations, serving custodial sentences or subject to diversionary or alternative measures.[396] In regard

---

[393] *Cf., e.g.,* CRC Committee, *Concluding Observations: Burkina Faso* (UN Doc. CRC/C/15/Add.193, 2002), para. 62.; more generally, *e.g.* CRC Committee, *Concluding Observations: Czech Republic* (UN Doc. CRC/C/15/Add.201, 2003), para. 66; for different aspects of deprivation of liberty in juvenile justice: *Concluding Observations: Moldova* (UN Doc. CRC/C/15/Add.192, 2002), para. 52.

[394] CRC Committee, *Day of General Discussion: State violence against children (22 September 2000),* UN Doc. CRC/C/97, para. 688, recs. 15, 16 and 24.

[395] 'Strengthen its efforts to educate and sensitise police personnel, judicial personnel and other staff within the justice system to the provisions of the Convention, especially concerning the special needs of children deprived of their liberty', *Concluding Observations: Jamaica* (UN Doc. CRC/C/15/Add.210, 2003), para. 57(c).

[396] CRC Committee, *Day of General Discussion: State violence against children (22 September 2000),* UN Doc. CRC/C/97, para. 688, rec. 14(b).

to Austria's State Party report, for example, the Committee has expressed concern about 'the lack of disaggregated statistics on types of offence, length of sentences, length of pre-trial detention, etc' and it requested further information on the situation of children in prison from the State Party.[397]

102. The crucial underlying aspect of the obligation to fulfil concerns the question of the establishment and maintenance of the necessary infrastructure and resources, interestingly an issue almost never touched upon by the Committee in the State reporting process in relation to deprivation of liberty.[398] This is particular unfortunate as efforts to take CRC standards seriously here would require an exceptionally strong commitment by States Parties to provide for alternative structures to detention, imprisonment or placement, usually involving highly specialised personnel and cost-intensive infrastructure (*e.g.* separate structures for adult and juvenile offenders), not to speak of promotional activities to challenge negative attitudes and prejudices in public opinion on children in conflict with the law, with their family etc.[399] In addition, reference should be made here to the general prohibition of retrogressive measures, depriving children of the core content of rights below standards already reached.[400] This could be argued here, for instance, in relation to the right of children to specialized treatment while deprived of their liberty, or to be kept separated from adults.[401]

103. Finally, a key question among provisional duties of the States Parties remains the issue of prevention of violations to the child's personal liberty and of disrespect for standards on deprivation of their liberty. Measures to be adopted here include, for instance, registration of all detained persons,[402] monitoring mechanisms[403] and internal effective (*i.e.* child-sensitive) complaint procedures to address

---

[397] CRC Committee, *Concluding Observations: Austria* (UN Doc. CRC/C/15/Add.98, 1999), para. 29.

[398] In the words of *Abramson*, on the juvenile justice, 'there is a notable absence in the Concluding Observations of the "M-word": money', B. Abramson, *o.c.* (note 247), I/2. On a more general level, the Committee addresses quite often the need of States Parties to seek international cooperation and technical assistance from various UN bodies for implementation of CRC standards.

[399] *Cf. Abramson* on the 'unpopularity' aspect of juvenile justice, B. Abramson, *o.c.* (note 247), I/1.

[400] M. Nowak, *Introduction to the International Human Rights Regime, o.c.* (note 382), p. 50. *Cf.* also the CESCR Committee in its standard-setting *General Comment No. 14 (2000) on the Right to Health, o.c.* (note 308), para. 32.

[401] On the importance of this standards, *cf.* B. Abramson, *o.c.* (note 247), I/2.

[402] Regarding India, the CRC Committee recommended, for instance, that 'registration of each child taken to a police station be mandatory, including time, date and reason for detention': CRC Committee, *Concluding Observations: India* (UN Doc. CRC/C/15/Add.115, 2000), para. 39.

[403] Curiously, concerning Liechtenstein the Committee asked for additional information on monitoring of children of that country detained in Austria, 'owing to the lack of facilities in the State party': CRC Committee, *Concluding Observations: Liechtenstein* (UN Doc. CRC/C/15/Add.143, 2001), para. 28.

violations of these standards[404] as well as investigation of abuse.[405] Only from time to time the Committee enters into some discussion on the underlying circumstances *e.g.* of children in conflict with the law, offering advice in relation to the Riyadh Guidelines on prevention of juvenile delinquency and calling *e.g.* for support of families and communities for improved social conditions.[406]

2.3   The CRC Context

104. The CRC calls for the adoption of a context-oriented child-focussed approach to all measures affecting children directly or indirectly, taking into account the continuously evolving capacities of the child.[407] In the following, therefore, a 'child personal liberty perspective' on the Convention will be adopted, providing for a brief overview of CRC provisions interpreted in the specific context of deprivation of liberty.

105. The CRC Committee has identified four general principles guiding interpretation and implementation of the whole Convention.[408] First, the CRC asks for realisation of all rights to all children without discrimination, under the jurisdiction of the State Party (Article 2(1)). In this regard two aspects may be distinguished: discrimination of children because of their status as being deprived of their liberty in relation to all other children (as a 'other status' group under Article 2(1), *e.g.* in regard to potential interferences with access to education, health care etc), and discrimination between various groups of children already deprived or likely to be deprived of their liberty. While the first aspect frames, in essence, the whole of the discussion here on Article 37, the second relates to more specific issues, such as heightened risk of certain groups of children to be arrested, detained, mistreated in detention etc.

106. In this regard, the CRC Committee repeatedly voiced concern about State legislation and practice affecting particular groups of children. In regard to Australia, the Committee criticized the 'unjustified, disproportionately high percentage of Aboriginal children in the juvenile justice system and that there is a tendency to

---

[404] *Cf.* CRC Committee, *Concluding Observations: Italy* (UN Doc. CRC/C/15/Add.198, 2003), para. 53(b): '[a]llow periodic visits to the Reception Centres and Penal Institutes for Minors by impartial and independent, child-sensitive and accessible complaint procedure'.

[405] 'Investigate, prosecute and punish any case of mistreatment committed by law enforcement personnel, including prison guards': CRC Committee, *Concluding Observations: Madagascar* (UN Doc. CRC/C/15/Add.218, 2003), para. 69(h).

[406] CRC Committee, *Concluding Observations: Moldova* (UN Doc. CRC/C/15/Add.192, 2002), para. 52(f); *Georgia* (UN Doc. CRC/C/15/Add.222, 2003), para. 69(d).

[407] Article 5 of the CRC for the family context; as a general principle of interpretation, *cf.* G. Van Bueren, *o.c.* (note 239), p. 45 *et seq.*

[408] CRC Committee, *General Comment No. 5 (2003) General measures of implementation for the Convention on the Rights of the Child, o.c.* (note 308), para. 12.

refuse applications for bail to them'.[409] Similarly, *vis-à-vis* Greece, the Committee expressed concern about the 'proportionally high number of children from distinct ethnic, religious, linguistic and cultural groups' in the juvenile justice system, 'especially involving arrest and imprisonment'.[410] In the cases of both Bulgaria and the Czech Republic, the Committee, within the context of juvenile justice and deprivation of liberty, remained 'particularly worried' about the 'stigmatization of the most vulnerable categories of children, including those belonging to the Roma minority.'[411] Furthermore the Committee was concerned about the 'increasing number of children placed in detention, disproportionately affecting children of foreign origin' in Germany,[412] and it asked the United Kingdom government to ensure 'that there is no discrimination in benefit entitlements for asylum-seeking families that could affect children'.[413] Turning to Latin America, the Committee found discrimination against children living in poverty, being discriminatorily affected by broad judicial powers in sentencing young persons.[414] Mention should also be made her of territorial limitations: the Committee recommended to India to '[e]xtend the application of the Juvenile Justice (Care and Protection of Children) Act, 2000, to the State of Jammu and Kashmir'.[415]

107. The situation of girls in relation to deprivation of liberty has not yet been systematically addressed by the CRC Committee; during the 1995 Day of General Discussion on the girl child, the only link offered relates to differences in the setting of the age of criminal responsibility. However, given prevailing general attitudes towards girls and imbalances of power, girls are particularly vulnerable to violence, abuse and exploitation particularly in closed settings like detention facilities and prisons, warranting a much more gender-focussed approach to deprivation of liberty.[416] For instance, the UN Special Rapporteur on violence against women

---

[409] CRC Committee, *Concluding Observations: Australia* (UN Doc. CRC/C/15/Add.79, 1997), para. 22. It voiced concern also about legislation in two Australian States (with high percentage of Aboriginal population) which provides in certain situations for mandatory detention of juveniles, again particularly affecting Aborigines.

[410] CRC Committee, *Concluding Observations: Greece* (UN Doc. CRC/C/15/Add.170, 2002), para. 78.

[411] CRC Committee, *Concluding Observations: Bulgaria* (UN Doc. CRC/C/15/Add.66, 1997), para. 19, and *Czech Republic* (UN Doc. CRC/C/15/Add.81, 1997), para. 25, with identical wording.

[412] CRC Committee, *Concluding Observations: Germany* (UN Doc. CRC/C/15/Add.226, 2004), para. 60.

[413] CRC Committee, *Concluding Observations: United Kingdom* (UN Doc. CRC/C/15/Add. 188, 2002), para. 50(b). In relation to migrants, the Special Rapporteur also states that they are 'particularly vulnerable to deprivation of liberty', as 'there is a tendency to criminalize violations of immigration regulations' and 'a great number of countries resort to administrative detention of irregular migrants pending deportation', UN Doc. E/CN.4/2003/85 (30 December 2002), p. 2.

[414] CRC Committee, *Concluding Observations: Bolivia* (UN Doc. CRC/C/15/Add.1, 1993), para. 11.

[415] CRC Committee, *Concluding Observations: India* (UN Doc. CRC/C/15/Add.228, 2004), para. 80(b).

[416] *Cf.* Rule 26.4 of the Beijing Rules; *cf.* also B. Abramson, *o.c.* (note 247), I/2.

highlighted the practice in some South Asian countries of 'protective custody' for women victims of trafficking: they are brought to 'government homes', confined to certain areas and staying sometimes 'for many years in these homes, forgotten by everyone'; accordingly, she concludes that '[p]rotective custody as practised in South Asia is a serious violation of women's rights'.[417]

108. The over-all guiding principle of the Convention—to give primary consideration to the best interests of children in all matters affecting them (directly or indirectly)—ensures principal child-orientation also in relation to deprivation of liberty of children. It bears relevance, for example, for the consideration of issues like cultural differences and their impact *e.g.* on detention practices and conditions.[418] Furthermore it ensures a child-focussed approach for the interpretation of complementary provisions of other human rights treaties not explicitly contained in the CRC but of relevance here (*e.g.* the right to compensation for unlawful deprivation of liberty, Article 9(5) of the CCPR); and the best interests clause provides a reliable treaty-based anchor for the integration of principles contained in nonbinding standards on deprivation of liberty, such as the 1990 JDL Rules.

109. Furthermore, key concepts of relevant non-binding UN standards, such as diversion,[419] the principle of proportionality of the reaction to child offenders[420] and not least the principles of last resort to and shortest period of time of deprivation of liberty,[421] finally incorporated into the CRC, could be regarded as concrete expressions of the best interests clause. Together with the CRC concept of respect for the evolving capacities of the child (Article 5), the best interests principle is also of crucial importance for interpretation and assessment of age limits (*e.g.* criminal responsibility) and treatment and conditions during deprivation of liberty—irrespective of *e.g.* a special juvenile justice system in place. As a consequence, no reservations to the best interests of the child as the CRC's most fundamental guarantee would be permissible.[422]

110. The best interests of the child principle is inextricably linked to the child's right to participation in all relevant matters (Article 12 of the CRC); this follows from the CRC's fundamental approach to the child as a subject on its own right, countering paternalistic or needs-centred attitudes to children by listening to them and taking actively into account the views of the child concerned. However, respect for this approach constitutes a crucial challenge especially in situations of depri-

---

[417] Report of the Special Rapporteur on violence against women, its causes and consequences: Mission to Bangladesh, Nepal and India on the issue of trafficking of women and girls (2000), UN Doc. E/CN.4/2001/73/Add.2 (6 February 2001), para. 28.
[418] J.W. Tobin, *o.c.* (note 322), p. 215.
[419] Rule 11 of the Beijing Rules.
[420] Rules 5 and 17 of the Beijing Rules.
[421] Rules 13.1 and 17.1(c) of the Beijing Rules, Rule 2 of the JDL Rules.
[422] *Cf.* Article 51(2) of the CRC, G. Van Bueren, *o.c.* (note 239), p. 51.

vation of liberty. Typically, and in addition to the difficult status of children in societies, the child, here, is in an even much weaker and more dependent position: it may have broken mainstream standards of society or even laws, facing criminal proceedings now, or it is an unaccompanied child refugee confronted with an official of the asylum authority who decides within the next five minutes on the legality of his or her future stay in that country. In such situations, safeguarding the child's right to be heard and taken seriously requires particularly strong commitment and action by all actors involved. Similarly, child-sensitivity and accessibility of complaint and review mechanisms (including Article 37(d)) should be assessed in light of Article 12 of the CRC.

111. The serious impact of interferences with the right to personal liberty on the child's right to life, survival and healthy development (Article 6) has already been stressed; and while deprivation of liberty still remains an accepted limitation justified under very specific circumstances, the basic principle has to be repeated that all other child rights have to be ensured to the utmost extent possible.[423] This applies equally to situations of children in police custody, pre-trial detention, imprisonment, detention pending deportation, children placed in closed psychiatric facilities or in 'correctional institutions.' However, reality is far from meeting these requirements and the principle of 'last resort' as contained in Article 37(b) second sentence of the CRC provides a clear mandate to reduce deprivation of the child's liberty to an absolute minimum, for exceptional cases only.[424]

112. Apart from the General Principles' significance for protecting the rights of children deprived of their liberty, as enshrined in Article 37(b), (c), (d), practically all other CRC provisions show direct bearing for these children. Evidently, there is an immediate link to Article 37(a), which contains specific qualifications both in regard to deprivation of liberty as a sentence under criminal law (prohibiting death penalty and life imprisonment without possibility of release, following the 'shortest period of time' rule of Article 37(b) second sentence) and to conditions and treatment during deprivation of liberty (prohibiting torture and other cruel, inhuman or degrading treatment or punishment, reflecting also Article 37(c)).[425] Similarly,

---

[423] *Cf.* Rule 1 of the JDL Rules: ' The juvenile justice system should uphold the rights and safety and promote the physical and mental well-being of juveniles'; Human Rights Committee, *General Comment No. 21 (1992): Replaces general comment 9 concerning humane treatment of persons deprived of liberty (Art. 10)*, *o.c.* (note 308), para. 3: 'Persons deprived of their liberty enjoy all the rights set forth in the Covenant, subject to the restrictions that are unavoidable in a closed environment'; G. Van Bueren, *o.c.* (note 239), p. 206: 'Individuals deprived of liberty are entitled to the enjoyment of all their rights under international law which are compatible with their deprivation of liberty'; or, just simply: '[People] are in prison as punishment, but not for punishment', Penal Reform International, *Making standards work—an international handbook on good prison practice* (second edition, The Hague, Penal Reform International, 2001), p. 6.

[424] Rule 2 of the JDL Rules, Rule 17.1(c) of the Beijing Rules.

[425] *Cf. supra* Part I.

CRC provisions on juvenile justice (Article 40) have direct impact on deprivation of liberty, including its over-all aim of reintegration of the child, standards for fair trial and its call for alternative measures to institutional placement. The juvenile justice concept of diversion correlates to the 'last resort'-principle of standards on deprivation of liberty. Finally, the CRC Committee in its concluding observations routinely adds to Articles 37 and 40 the obligations of States Parties under Article 39, providing for physical and psychological recovery and rehabilitation of the child victim of violence and exploitation.[426]

113. Issues of concern for the child's personal liberty, furthermore, may arise in institutional settings under a child and youth welfare regime, with children outside their family environment placed in alternative care arrangements (Article 20, see also Article 3(3));[427] Article 25 guarantees a specific right of the child to periodic review of his or her placement 'for the purpose of care, protection or treatment of his or her physical or mental health'. In addition, Article 23 requires inclusive services adapted to the needs of children with disabilities—another challenging area for implementation of standards on deprivation of liberty;[428] Article 22 provides for provisional duties of the State Party to ensure 'appropriate protection and humanitarian assistance' to child refugees.[429]

114. The right to education and the right to health require particular attention within the context of children deprived of their liberty. Children and young persons below the age of 18 should receive education; or they may have already started a job. Any form of detention or placement in a closed institution leads to an interruption of these developments and standards on deprivation of liberty require comprehensive measures for compensation. Accordingly, the JDL Rules devote an entire sub-chapter (IV.E) to matters of 'education, vocational training and work', acknowledging that every child 'of compulsory school age has the right to education suited to his or her needs and abilities and designed to prepare him or her for return to society' (Rule 38). Moreover, the Rules state that education 'should be provided outside the detention facility in community schools wherever possible', continuing with more detailed standards on availability and quality of educational and

---

[426] Interestingly, during the drafting of Article 39 the representative of Argentina—unsuccessfully—proposed to include 'imprisonment' in the list of situations contained in Article 39 requiring child rehabilitation, UN Doc. E/CN.4/1989/48, para. 529.

[427] On the other hand, the Convention also protects family relations by providing safeguards against arbitrary separation of the child from his or her parents; and more specifically, Article 9(4) poses a duty on States Parties to provide both parents or the child with information about the whereabouts of the relatives, if the separation resulted from a State action, such as detention or imprisonment.

[428] *Cf.* Rule 4 of the JDL Rules, prohibiting discrimination based, *inter alia*, on disability, and Rule 38: 'Juveniles who are illiterate or have cognitive or learning difficulties should have the right to special education'; similarly, *cf.* Rules 13 and 26 of the Beijing Rules.

[429] On detention of child refugees, *cf. infra* Part II, Chapter III/2.5.

vocational training programmes and work opportunities.[430] The CRC Committee has addressed access to education while in detention, expressing, for instance, its strong concern towards the United Kingdom's government that 'children deprived of their liberty in prisons and juvenile detention centres do not have the statutory right to education'.[431] Related to educational services and opportunities for meaningful work the CRC right to rest and leisure, play and recreation (Article 31) is often over-looked. Rule 47 of the JDL Rules further elaborates on a broad range of measures to be taken by the authorities in this regard, including availability of space and services for daily free exercises, sports, arts and crafts skill development.

115. Similarly, access to medical services is of utmost importance to children deprived of their liberty. Again, sub-chapter IV.H of the JDL Rules provide far-reaching standards in relation to the right to health: 'Every juvenile shall receive adequate medical care, both preventive and remedial, including dental, ophthalmological and mental health care, as well as pharmaceutical products and special diets as medically indicated' (Rule 49).[432] The CRC Committee has both in its 1998 Day of General Discussion and in its 2003 General Comment on HIV/AIDS highlighted the particular vulnerability of children deprived of their liberty to effects of this disease.[433] In the State report monitoring process, the Committee occasionally refers to problems in granting access to health services; in relation to Burkina Faso, for example, the Committee recommended within the juvenile justice context to '[i]ntroduce regular medical examination of children by independent medical staff'.[434]

116. Finally, a cross-cutting 'child personal liberty' approach to the CRC has, of course, to take into account various protective rights and standards,[435] including protection of the child's privacy (Article 16 of the CRC) as well as protection from all forms of violence (Article 19) and exploitation (Articles 32 *et seq.*). Rules 87(d) and (e) of the JDL Rules consequently provide in relation to duties of personnel to 'ensure the full protection of the physical and mental health of juveniles, including protection from physical, sexual and emotional abuse and exploitation'[436] and

---

[430] *Cf.* also Rules 13, 24 and 26 of the Beijing Rules on educational services.

[431] CRC Committee, *Concluding Observations: the United Kingdom* (UN Doc. CRC/C/15/Add.188, 2002), para. 47.

[432] The CESCR Committee in its *General Comment No. 14 (2000) on the right to health* expressly held that 'States are under the obligation to respect the right to health by, *inter alia*, refraining from denying or limiting equal access for all persons, including prisoners or detainees', *o.c.* (note 308), para. 34.

[433] CRC Committee, *Day of General Discussion: HIV/AIDS (5 October 1998)*, UN Doc. CRC/C/80, para. 243(l) and *General Comment No. 3 (2003)*, *o.c.* (note 308), para. 30.

[434] CRC Committee, *Concluding Observations: Burkina Faso* (UN Doc. CRC/C/15/Add.193, 2002), para. 62(i).

[435] *Cf.* also related standards on alternative care (Articles 20, 21), periodic review of treatment while in care (Article 25) and quality standards for child welfare facilities (Article 3(3)), *cf.* also S. Detrick, *o.c.* (note 253), p. 326.

[436] *Cf.* also Rule 8 on protection of privacy and Rule 10.3 of the Beijing Rules: 'Contacts

to 'respect the right of the juvenile to privacy, and, in particular, [to] safeguard all confidential matters concerning juveniles or their families learned as a result of their professional capacity'. In relation to violence it should be stated that respective managing authorities of detention centres, prisons and other institutions hosting children fall under the scope of 'any other person who has the care of the child' of Article 19. Thus this provision qualifies and reinforces the wide-ranging protective responsibilities already contained in Article 37(c) (treatment with respect for the child's dignity) and Article 37(a) (prohibition of torture).[437]

2.4   Legality and Non-Arbitrariness

117. Article 37(b) straightforwardly obliges States Parties to ensure that: 'No child shall be deprived of his or her liberty unlawfully or arbitrarily.' The wording bears strong resemblance to Article 9(1) of the CCPR, which served as the template for the CRC text,[438] while clarifying that under the CRC all forms of deprivation of liberty have to pass the double-test of lawfulness and non-arbitrariness for justification. Both requirements have a distinct meaning[439] and have to be met cumulatively. In short, 'lawful' addresses compliance with the grounds and procedures set primarily under domestic law for deprivation of liberty, whereas 'non-arbitrary' adds elements beyond the principle of legality, including reasonableness of the law itself and proportionality of measures.

118. During the drafting of this paragraph there was almost no discussion about the first sentence; Canada explained in the introduction (to the whole paragraph (b)) the intention to reflect both the CCPR and Beijing Rules standards, and Italy suggested to include at the end of the first sentence the additional CCPR wording of 'except on the grounds and in accordance with such procedure as are established by law', but did not insist on their proposal and the text was adopted as final by consensus.[440] For an understanding of the 'lawfulness' criterion it is therefore valuable to look at the comparable CCPR discussion. There, during the drafting of Article 9 of the CCPR, the lawfulness requirement was introduced 'as an alterna-

---

between the law enforcement agencies and a juvenile offender shall be managed in such a way as to respect the legal status of the juvenile, promote the well-being of the juvenile and avoid harm to her or him, with due regard to the circumstances of the case'.

[437] The UN Study on Violence against children requested by the UN General Assembly in 2001 will also address violence in detention facilities, prisons and generally in the administration of justice, *cf.* the 2003 concept paper by the independent expert to conduct the study, Paulo Sergio Pinheiro, contained in UN Doc. E/CN.4/2004/68, annex, para. 11; *cf.* also the recommendations of the CRC Committee, *Day of General Discussion: State violence against children (22 September 2000)*, UN Doc. CRC/C/97, para. 688.

[438] *Cf.* S. Detrick, *o.c.* (note 253), p. 629. For an interpretation of the much less clear-cut wording of the CCPR, *cf.* M. Nowak, *o.c.* (note 255), Article 9, para. 17 *et seq.*

[439] *Cf.* M. Nowak, *o.c.* (note 255), Article 9, para. 28.

[440] UN Doc. E/CN.4/1989/48, para. 547.

tive to an exhaustive listing of all permissible cases of deprivation of liberty', with a clear focus on the domestic legal system.[441] It refers to the grounds for deprivation of liberty and for the procedure to follow in its execution. Moreover, according to Nowak, 'law' in this sense rather narrowly refers to 'a general-abstract, parliamentary statute or an equivalent, unwritten norm of common law accessible to all individuals subject to the relevant jurisdiction'; administrative provisions provide sufficient basis for deprivations of liberty only if 'taken in enforcement of a law that provides for such interference with adequate clarity' and which 'regulates the procedure to be observed'.[442] As a consequence, any deprivation of liberty necessitates both legislation and clear competences for the executive in order to comply with the lawfulness requirement.

119. This understanding is also reflected in statements by the CRC Committee; in its Concluding Observations on Kazakhstan's State report, the Committee expressed concern about 'the existence of subordinate norms and departmental regulations and instructions that allow the restriction of freedom of children without fully complying with the provisions of the criminal, criminal-procedural and criminal-executive legislation'.[443] Interestingly, in its ensuing recommendation to the Kazakh government, the Committee advised to '[e]nsure that existing norms and regulations allowing the restriction of freedom of children conform to the laws of Kazakhstan *and international standards*'.[444] Here, the CRC Committee follows a development seen with other international human rights monitoring bodies as well: in cases on mandatory detention of immigrants and asylum-seekers, the Human Rights Committee decided that domestic provisions have to include compatibility with international law (including the CCPR itself) for passing the specific lawfulness test.[445]

---

[441] *Cf.* M. Nowak, *o.c.* (note 255), Article 9, para. 26 and 27; see, however, the different approach taken by Article 5 of the ECHR, *cf. supra* Part II, Chapter II.

[442] *Cf.* M. Nowak, *o.c.* (note 255), Article 9, para. 27.

[443] CRC Committee, *Concluding Observations: Kazakhstan* (UN Doc. CRC/C/15/Add.213, 2003), para. 66(f).

[444] *Emphasis added*, CRC Committee, *Concluding Observations: Kazakhstan* (UN Doc. CRC/C/15/Add.213, 2003), para. 67(d).

[445] *Cf.* M. Nowak, *o.c.* (note 255), Article 9, para. 27, with further references to case-law; *cf.* in this regard the similar approach by the UN Working Group on Arbitrary Detention, not least in relation to Australia again: Report of the Working Group on Arbitrary Detention—Visit to Australia, UN Doc. E/CN.4/2003/8/Add.2 (24 October 2002), paras. 23–27. Still, the specific lawfulness requirement should not be confused with the over-all obligation of States Parties to comply with standards contained in the respective international treaty. The European Court on Human Rights, in the *Winterwerp v. The Netherlands* case held in 1979 that '[t]he Court for its part considers that the words "in accordance with a procedure prescribed by law" essentially refer back to domestic law; they state the need for compliance with the relevant procedure under that law. However, the domestic law must itself be in conformity with the Convention, including the general principles expressed or implied therein', Series A 33 (24 October 1979), para. 45; *cf. also* J.W. Tobin, *o.c.* (note 322), p. 219.

120. In relation to Article 37(b), it should be noted, moreover, that compliance with the lawfulness criterion and issues of 'grounds and procedure' of deprivation of liberty also includes the further qualification by the twin principles of using such measures as a last resort and for the shortest appropriate period of time only (Article 37(b) second sentence). This follows from the principal objective to generally restrict interferences with personal liberty of children,[446] which implies the need for a review of both the grounds for arrest, detention, imprisonment etc and the way of their application. As a result, domestic legislation which does not reflect the principles of 'last resort' and 'shortest appropriate period of time' does not comply with the requirement of lawfulness under Article 37(b) first sentence.

121. Unfortunately, the Committee does not regularly refer explicitly to the different requirements under Article 37(b). Using the monitoring process *vis-à-vis* Kazakhstan as an example again, there was no open mentioning of the principle of lawfulness under Article 37(b), but still the Committee cited as a 'shortcoming' in the juvenile justice system 'vague legal provisions', for the issuance, of decisions on the 'placement of children aged 11 to 14 in 'special educational institutions' as a form of punishment under criminal law; and in a similar vein, it criticized the 'placement of children from 3 to 18 in centres for temporary isolation, adaptation and rehabilitation for juveniles [. . .], without legal grounds or procedure'.[447] In relation to Myanmar, the Committee called on the government to 'limit by law the length of pre-trail detention'.[448] In a related area, the CRC Committee sometimes highlighted the importance of ensuring 'the full independence and impartiality of the judiciary' for protecting the rights of children deprived of their liberty.[449]

122. Furthermore, while not explicitly addressed by the CRC, the question of lawfulness also shows relevance to the matter of compensation. Under Article 9(5) of the CCPR, '[a]nyone who has been the victim of unlawful arrest or detention shall have an enforceable right to compensation'; this remedy, consequently, is guaranteed to children as well (provided that the respective State has ratified the CCPR). Nowak observes that this right is provided irrespective of an actual finding of a

---

[446] Beijing Rules, Rule 13 on detention pending trial, Rule 17 on adjudication; JDL Rules, Rule 2 on all forms of deprivation of liberty.

[447] CRC Committee, *Concluding Observations: Kazakhstan* (UN Doc. CRC/C/15/Add.213, 2003), paras. 66(c) and (d). The Netherlands was reminded to set a maximum limit for detention of children in their territory of Aruba, *Concluding Observations: The Netherlands* (UN Doc. CRC/C/15/Add.227, 2004), para. 59(b).

[448] CRC Committee, *Concluding Observations: Myanmar* (UN Doc. CRC/C/15/Add.237, 2004), para. 78(e).

[449] *Cf., e.g.*, CRC Committee, *Concluding Observations: Lao People's Democratic Republic* (UN Doc. CRC/C/15/Add.78, 1997), paras. 29 and 53; *Lebanon* (UN Doc. CRC/C/15/Add.54, 1996), para. 44; *Mauritius* (UN Doc. CRC/C/15/Add.64, 1996), 32; *Mongolia* (UN Doc. CRC/C/15/Add.48, 1996), para. 29.

violation of the right to personal liberty, it suffices to establish that the measure taken was unlawful.[450]

123. The prohibition of arbitrariness is sometimes used rather as an umbrella for all forms of non-permissible deprivation of liberty.[451] However, as already noted above, it adds an additional and distinct dimension to the requirement of lawfulness of deprivation of liberty and should therefore given due regard in assessing interferences with personal liberty. The requirement on non-arbitrary interference is 'directed at both the national legislature and the organs of enforcement'.[452] As Nowak further comments, it 'is not enough for deprivation of liberty to be provided for by law. The law itself must not be arbitrary, and the enforcement of the law in a given case must not take place arbitrarily'.[453] Substantially, this means that '[c]ases of deprivation of liberty provided for by the law must not be manifestly unproportional, unjust or unpredictable, and the specific manner in which an arrest is made must not be discriminatory and must be able to be deemed appropriate and proportional in view of the circumstances of the case.'[454] The Human Rights Committee, as far as Article 12(4) of the CCPR ('No one shall be arbitrarily deprived of the right to enter his own country') is concerned, noted that '[t]the reference to the concept of arbitrariness in this context is intended to emphasize that it applies to all State action, legislative, administrative and judicial; it guarantees that even interference provided for by law should be in accordance with the provisions, aims and objectives of the Covenant and should be, in any event, reasonable in the particular circumstances.'[455]

124. As a general rule, even if based on lawful grounds under domestic law, situations like political arrest or detention,[456] *incommunicado* detention, enforced disappearance

---

[450] *Cf.* M. Nowak, *o.c.* (note 255), Article 9, para. 54, with further references.
[451] *Cf.* Article 9 of the UDHR: No one shall be subjected to arbitrary arrest, detention or exile; *cf.* also the establishment of the UN Working Group on Arbitrary Detention.
[452] M. Nowak, *o.c.* (note 255), Article 9, para. 28.
[453] *Ibid.*, para. 28.
[454] *Ibid.*, para. 30.
[455] Human Rights Committee, *General Comment No. 27 (1999) : Freedom of movement (Art. 12)*, *o.c.* (note 308), para. 21.
[456] *Cf.* also three legal categories of arbitrary detention established by the UN Working Group on Arbitrary Detention, *supra* Part II, Chapter II/1: (a) When it is clearly impossible to invoke any legal basis justifying the deprivation of liberty (as when a person is kept in detention after the completion of his sentence or despite an amnesty law applicable to him) (category I); (b) When the deprivation of liberty results from the exercise of the rights or freedoms guaranteed by articles 7, 13, 14, 18, 19, 20 and 21 of the Universal Declaration of Human Rights and, insofar as States parties are concerned, by articles 12, 18, 19, 21, 22, 25, 26 and 27 of the International Covenant on Civil and Political Rights (category II); (c) When the total or partial non-observance of the international norms relating to the right to a fair trial, established in the Universal Declaration of Human Rights and in the relevant international instruments accepted by the States concerned, is of such gravity as to give the deprivation of liberty an arbitrary character (category III); UN Doc. E/CN.4/1998/44 (19 December 1997), Annex 1, para. 8.

or kidnappings by secret service agents constitute examples of arbitrary deprivation of liberty.[457] Similarly, detention initially lawful may become arbitrary if circumstances change or after prolonged continuation without justification,[458] including
continued detention despite order to release.

125. As stated before, the CRC Committee does not regularly draw a distinction
between lawfulness and arbitrariness when expressing concern about disregard for
standards on deprivation of liberty. In regard to the report of Indonesia, still, the
Committee was concerned about the situation of street children and 'at the violence to which they are subject, especially during sweep operations'; for this reason, it recommended to the government to 'end the violence, arbitrary arrest and
detention carried out by the State apparatus against street children'.[459] In the case
of Nigeria, the Committee boldly stated that 'current legislation with regard to the
administration of juvenile justice and the institutionalization of children does not
appear to conform to the principles and provisions of the Convention.' More specifically, it raised the issue of detention 'at Her Majesty's Pleasure', which 'may per-
mit the indiscriminate sentencing of children for indeterminate periods'. The same
matter came up in relation to the United Kingdom in cases before the European
Court on Human Rights.[460] In those cases involving the two young boys aged 10
who killed a two year old child, they were convicted of murder and sentenced to
detention 'during Her Majesty's pleasure', meaning that no specific length of detention was set, but instead it remained at the discretion of the British Home Secretary
to determine that period. Still, the ECtHR did not view this provision allowing for
indeterminate sentences as a violation of Article 5(1) nor as a violation of Article
3 (prohibition of inhuman or degrading treatment—by a narrow majority of 10 to
7 judges), but only a violation of judicial review under Article 5(4) of the ECHR (and
Article 6 in relation to the mandate of the Home Secretary). The CRC Committee,
however, in a related situation in Zambia, unmistakably declared it is 'deeply concerned that a child may be sentenced at the President's pleasure' and plainly called
for the prohibition of this penalty.[461] Similarly, the Committee recommended abol-

---

[457] M. Nowak, o.c. (note 255), Article 9, paras. 33, 34, with references to Human Rights
Committee case-law.
[458] Cf. the case A. v. Australia, Communication No. 560/1993, UN Doc. CCPR/C/59/D/560/1993
(3 April 1997): detention of persons seeking asylum was not per se considered arbitrary, but
prolonged detention for more than four years without proper possibility for review did render the detention arbitrary, para. 9.4; cf. M. Nowak, o.c. (note 255), Article 9, para. 33.
[459] CRC Committee, Concluding Observations: Indonesia (UN Doc. CRC/C/15/Add.223, 2004),
paras. 79 and 80(a). Cf. also Concluding Observations: Bangladesh (UN Doc. CRC/C/15/Add.74,
1997), para. 26: here the Committee showed concern for 'grounds of arrest and detention
that can include prostitution, "vagrancy" or "uncontrollable behaviour"'.
[460] Cf. ECtHR, T. (Application no. 24724/94) and V. (Application no. 24888/94) v. the United Kingdom,
16 December 1999, Reports 1999.
[461] CRC Committee, Concluding Observations: Zambia (UN Doc. CRC/C/15/Add.206, 2003),
paras. 70, 72(a). Cf. supra No. 42.

ishment of the Haitian legislation allowing parents to send children to prison for up to six months, 'without the involvement of a court or similar body'. Nevertheless it declared this a violation of Article 37(d) only, and not Article 37(b).[462]

2.5 *"As a measure of last resort" and*
"for the shortest appropriate period of time"

126. Article 37(b) second sentence contains the two most significant concepts in international treaty law on deprivation of liberty of children, by incorporating international non-binding standards on interferences 'only as a measure of last resort and for the shortest appropriate period of time'. This State obligation calls for a comprehensive understanding of the child's personal development, its interaction with his or her environment and others, before considering social reaction to a certain behaviour of the child. As expressed in the Riyadh Guidelines, 'youthful behaviour or conduct that does not conform to overall social norms and values is often part of the maturation and growth process' (Para. 5(g)). This applies to all kinds of situations, be it a conflict within the family between parents and the child, truant children refusing to go to school or crimes committed by a young person. As far as conflict with the law is concerned, the specific system of juvenile justice focuses on this process of the child's development, and in deciding on its reaction, it tries to keep the potential negative impact of intervention as small as possible. Therefore, the Beijing Rules state as their overall objective the well-being of the child and the application of the principle of proportionality in regard to any reaction to offences committed (Rules 5 and 17(1)); similarly, the concept of diversion (Rule 11) aims at hindering 'the negative effects of subsequent proceedings in juvenile justice administration (for example the stigma of conviction and sentence)'.[463] Deprivation of liberty, now, as a punishment constitutes one possible social reaction to a child in conflict with the law, but certainly one with the most serious impact on the child's development and its personal future. Therefore, the Beijing Rules, the JDL Rules and other documents[464] require authorities to first look for alternative measures to deprivation of liberty at all stages of the process or, at least, keep the period of time to a minimum,[465] when considering pre-trial

---

[462] CRC Committee, *Concluding Observations: Haiti* (UN Doc. CRC/C/15/Add.202, 2003), paras. 28, 29.

[463] Beijing Rules, Commentary on Rule 11.

[464] *Cf.*, in particular, the 1990 United Nations Standard Minimum Rules for Non-custodial Measures (The Tokyo Rules), stating in its preamble that 'alternatives to imprisonment can be an effective means of treating offenders within the community to the best advantage of both the offenders and the society'.

[465] With Rule 2 of the JDL Rules as the most comprehensive expression of this two-fold restriction on the use of deprivation of liberty in quantity and in time, *cf.* the Beijing Rules, Commentary on Rule 19.

detention[466] or imprisonment[467] or institutionalization.[468] This implies that mandatory pre-trial detention and sentencing of children is not compatible with Article
37(b) of the CRC, because it ignores the principle of proportionality and the discretion necessary for the decision in the individual case.[469]

127. By incorporating those standards, Article 37(b) of the CRC may serve as one
example of added value by the CRC towards child rights protection, as it does not
simply repeat existing standards but develops them further; unfortunately, however, this incorporation is not fully consistent. Already Article 9(3) of the CCPR
determines in relation to pre-trial detention that 'it shall not be the general rule
that persons awaiting trial shall be detained in custody', thus calling for the provision of bail and other guarantees to secure appearance for trail without recourse
to deprivation of liberty. More clearly, and with direct orientation towards children, these principles have been stated by Rule 13(1) of the Beijing Rules: 'Detention
pending trial shall be used only as a measure of last resort and for the shortest
possible period of time'. In its 'Guiding principles in adjudication and disposition'
Rules 17(1)(b) and (c), moreover, require the competent authority to take into
account that '[r]estrictions on the personal liberty of the juvenile shall be imposed
only after careful consideration and shall be limited to the possible minimum' and
continuing by declaring that '[d]eprivation of personal liberty shall not be imposed
unless the juvenile is adjudicated of a serious act involving violence against another
person or of persistence in committing other serious offences and unless there is
no other appropriate response'. Rule 2 of the JDL Rules, finally, proclaims the most
comprehensive formulation of these principles, covering not just arrest, detention
or imprisonment in a criminal justice context, but any placement of a child in a
lock-up setting:[470]

> 'Deprivation of the liberty of a juvenile should be a disposition of last resort and for
> the minimum necessary period and should be limited to exceptional cases.'

128. The extension of the scope of application to any 'placement of children in
closed institutions' was later confirmed by the 1997 Guidelines for Action on Children
in the Criminal Justice System, stating that '[s]uch placement of children should
only take place in accordance with the provisions of article 37(b) of the Convention
and as a matter of last resort and for the shortest period of time' (para. 18).

---

[466] Rule 13 of the Beijing Rules, Rule 17 of the JDL Rules.
[467] Rule 17 of the Beijing Rules, Rule 1 of the JDL Rules.
[468] Rule 19 of the Beijing Rules. *Cf.* also the Recommendations of the Day of General
Discussion on State violence against children, with the Committee recommending 'that penal
legislation applicable to juveniles be reviewed so as to ensure that courts are not restricted
to custodial sentences disproportionate to the offence', *Day of General Discussion: State violence
against children (22 September 2000)*, UN Doc. CRC/C/97, para. 688.
[469] *Cf.* also, B. Abramson, *o.c.* (note 247), I/2.
[470] *Cf.* Rule 11(b) for the JDL Rules' scope of application.

129. It is striking in this development, however, that Article 37(b) of the CRC itself does not speak of 'deprivation of liberty' here, but only refers to 'arrest, detention or imprisonment', thus leaving out other forms of placement outside the criminal/juvenile justice context. This is particularly remarkable, as the CRC, in all other provisions of Article 37, uses the broader notion of 'deprivation of liberty' as a point of reference. The drafting history reveals[471] that the second sentence of Article 37(b) was subject of a very controversial debate in the plenary working group. The initial draft proposed by an informal sub-working group consistently referred to deprivation of liberty throughout the article. And while the first sentence of Article 37(b) was passed without major discussion, heated debate around the second sentence arose. Delegates from Kuwait and the USSR strongly voiced concerns that by adopting these principles 'the Working Group would be deciding on detailed measures of juvenile punishment without the necessary expertise to do so'.[472] In particular, the USSR representative questioned 'whether it was the consensus view of experts on juvenile punishment' that deprivation of liberty should be restricted to the shortest possible period of time.[473] Similarly, the representative of the Federal Republic of Germany opposed the proposal by referring to domestic legislation on custodial sentences which did not include the time limitation. Italy, then, proposed deletion of the second sentence, while Senegal defended its inclusion 'in order to encourage judges to consider the use of other educational or correctional measures than deprivation of liberty and to ensure that, if at all, custodial measures would only be used as a measure of last resort'.[474] Others proposed the deletion of the limitation on time, until finally, at this stage of the discussion, the USSR representative suggested 'that the broad notion of "deprivation of liberty" be replaced by the more precise words "imprisonment, arrest and detention" and that the text should indicate that the measures should be "in conformity with the law"'.[475] This proposal attracted most support in the end,[476] with the USSR, Senegal, the United States and the German Democratic Republic finally stating 'their preference for a more specific language instead of a general reference such as "deprivation of liberty", since this term could also cover educational and other types of deprivation of liberty applied to minors besides detention, arrest, or imprisonment'.[477] With a last amendment in order to accommodate concerns about the time limitation (replacing 'shortest possible' by 'shortest appropriate period of time'), the second sentence was finally adopted.[478] And as a result, Van Bueren concludes that 'States

---

[471] *Cf. supra* Part II, Chapter III/1.
[472] UN Doc. E/CN.4/1989/48, para. 549.
[473] *Ibid.*, para. 549.
[474] *Ibid.*, para. 550.
[475] *Ibid.*, para. 551.
[476] With the French delegate still questioning the need for one more reference to conformity with the law, as 'the word "unlawfully" which was contained in the first sentence adequately met any concerns which the phrase was intended to cover', *ibid.*, para. 553.
[477] *Ibid.*, para. 556.
[478] *Ibid.*, para. 560.

Parties to the CRC are therefore under a duty only to impose arrest, imprisonment and detention as a measure of last resort rather than all forms of deprivation of liberty.'[479]

130. However, such restrictive interpretation would not adequately take into account the context and purpose of CRC standards in this regard. The brief drafting account above has demonstrated the compromise character of the second sentence of Article 37(b), in light of the consensus principle adopted by the drafting Working Group.[480] It reflects the status of the international debate at that time insofar, as on the one hand, important standard-setting initiatives in the field of juvenile justice and related areas such as deprivation of liberty took place at the end of the 1980s, while, on the other hand, some governments were not prepared to adopt the new principles already in their domestic legal system at that time. For the sake of consensus, therefore, the 1989 CRC text only refers to arrest, detention and imprisonment in the context of the 'last resort/shortest period of time' principles as the lowest common denominator, then. However, only one year later, the JDL Rules were adopted without a vote by the General Assembly, and the JDL Rules deliberately do not limit those two principles to the criminal justice context, but make them applicable to any form of placement depriving children of their personal liberty (*e.g.* for children with 'difficult behaviour' under a child social welfare regime). In fact, it should be seen as one of the key achievements of the JDL Rules that they have overcome the traditional narrow perception of deprivation of liberty as a criminal justice issue only. This development should not be jeopardized by maintaining more restrictive standards under the CRC adopted at an earlier time.[481] Apart from that, Van Bueren herself calls on the CRC Committee to 'use the Rules for the Protection of Juveniles Deprived of their Liberty as a normative framework',[482] and as already explained earlier, the Committee does in fact apply the JDL Rules in its work.

131. Moreover, all the arguments in relation to the severe impact of limitations to the child's personal liberty and his or her development are valid irrespective of the legal regime ordering such measure. Also, looking at purposes of deprivation of liberty, there is the clear focus on rehabilitation in the juvenile justice area. This should also be accepted for other purposes, like educational considerations or public or the individual's personal safety. Applying the 'last resort/shortest period of time' principles here would include again the requirement to pass the double-test of whether the intended deprivation of liberty is really the one last option (without any alternatives less interfering with the child's right) and if 'yes', what would

---

[479] G. Van Bueren, *o.c.* (note 239), p. 209.
[480] S. Detrick, *o.c.* (note 252), p. 20.
[481] It would mean, *e.g.* for the CRC Committee to apply JDL Rules standards in general to all forms of deprivation of liberty, but limit some of their most important principles to just one specific context out of its broader scope of application.
[482] G. Van Bueren, *o.c.* (note 239), p. 211.

be an appropriate time frame, with the implicit duty to regularly review the situation and consider its continued justification.[483] Applying the two principles basically shifts the burden of proof for authorities to argue why—as an exceptional measure—deprivation of liberty is necessary, first (*i.e.* assess all available alternatives), and still necessary (*i.e.* not inappropriately prolonged), second. If these principles are well-established for the field of juvenile justice, it would not be compatible with the object and purpose (Article 31(1) of the Vienna Convention on the Law of Treaties) of over-all CRC standards on deprivation of liberty and in light of succeeding developments of standards to exclude other forms of deprivation of liberty from its application. Article 37(b) second sentence should be interpreted in a way that specific forms of deprivation of liberty are expressly referred to as being guided by the 'last resort/shortest period of time'-principles, but only as a minimum, and not limited to arrest, detention or imprisonment.

132. The CRC Committee's position on the scope of applicability of Article 37(b) second sentence is not yet clarified. On the one hand it has accepted the JDL definition of deprivation of liberty for its Periodic Reporting Guidelines, it routinely recommends States Parties to implement the JDL Rules and it frequently refers to the principles of last resort and shortest period of time, then; on the other hand most of these discussions on deprivation of liberty take place in the juvenile justice context. On a very general level, the 1995 Day of General Discussion of the CRC Committee on the Administration of Juvenile Justice stated that the CRC 'called for the implementation of the most conducive provisions for the realization of the rights of the child, and had therefore to be considered in conjunction with other relevant international instruments, namely the Beijing Rules, the Riyadh Guidelines and the Rules for the Protection of Juveniles Deprived of their Liberty'.[484] In fact, the CRC Committee has expressed concern over disrespect for the principles of last resort and shortest period of time on many occasions, extending also beyond the juvenile justice context.[485]

133. One such particular issue relates to detention of asylum-seeking refugee children. It is quite frequent for children applying for asylum in wealthier reception countries to be taken into administrative detention during parts or whole of the asylum procedure. Many of these children are even separated from their parents, which leaves them in a particularly vulnerable and dependent situation upon their arrival. In such circumstances to be additionally kept in a closed location, in an

---

[483] *Cf.* similarly, Art. 25 of the CRC.

[484] CRC Committee, *Day of General Discussion on the Administration of Juvenile Justice (13th November 1995)*, UN Doc. CRC/C/43, 1995, para. 214.

[485] Nepal, for instance, was criticized by the Committee for its treatment of children with mental disabilities, with legislation allowing 'mentally ill children to be put in jail and chained', *Concluding Observations: Nepal* (UN Doc. CRC/C/15/Add.57, 1996), para. 24. *Cf.* also the following on administrative detention for child refugees.

unknown country, with frequent contact by police and security organs certainly
does not create a setting for 'appropriate protection and humanitarian assistance',
as mandated by Article 22 of the CRC. Moreover, considering standards on deprivation of liberty, Rule 17(1) of the Beijing Rules states, '[d]eprivation of liberty shall
not be imposed unless the juvenile is adjudicated of a serious act involving violence against another person or of persistence in committing other serious offences
and unless there is no other appropriate response'. If such a standard is required
for application in juvenile justice field, then the mere disregard of administrative
provisions (like unlawful entry into the country by the refugee), certainly cannot
justify administrative detention of child refugees, under the principle of last resort.
Instead, authorities should focus on less intrusive alternative measures, allowing
for adequate accommodation, access to education, health and meaningful occupation.

134. Consequently, the Office of the UN High Commissioner for Refugees, for example, has issued statements and guidelines already since 1988 declaring that child
refugees should not be detained, echoed by a wide range of international agencies
and non-governmental organisations.[486] The CRC Committee has also addressed the
issue of detention of child refugees, outside the context of juvenile justice, in rather
strong words. In respect to the situation in Austria, the Committee declared in 1999
that '[n]otwithstanding the 1997 Alien's Act requirement to use "more lenient means
when minors are involved", the Committee is seriously concerned about legislation which permits the detention of asylum-seeking children pending deportation'
and it goes on to 'urge the State party to reconsider the practice of detaining
asylum-seeking children, and that such children be treated in accordance with the
best interests of the child and in the light of the provisions of articles 20 and 22 of
the Convention'.[487] Under the heading 'special protection measures', subsection
'asylum-seeking/refugee children', the Committee also assessed the situation of
asylum-seeking children in the United Kingdom in 2002; here, it explicitly expressed
its concern that 'detention of these children is incompatible with the principles
and provisions of the Convention';[488] moreover, it criticized that 'processing appli-

---

[486] Cf. chapter 7 ('Personal liberty and security') of UNHCR, *Refugee Children—Guidelines on
Protection and Care* (Geneva, UNHCR, 1994); UNHCR, *Guidelines on Policies and Procedures in deal-
ing with Unaccompanied Children Seeking Asylum* (Geneva, UNHCR, 1997), para. 7.6–7.8; UNHCR,
Revised Guidelines on Applicable Criteria and Standards Relating to the Detention of Asylum Seekers
(Geneva, UNHCR, 1999), Guideline 6: 'Detention of Persons under the Age of 18 years: In
accordance with the general principle stated at Guideline 2 and the UNHCR Guidelines on
Refugee Children, minors who are asylum-seekers should not be detained'; most recently,
cf. the *Inter-agency Guiding Principles on unaccompanied and separated children*, p. 60, issued in
2004 by UNICEF, UNHCR, International Committee of the Red Cross, International Rescue
Committee, World Vision International and Save the Children UK. Cf. also the references to
the UN Working Group on Arbitrary Detention and other relevant monitoring mechanisms,
supra Part II, Chapter II.1.
[487] CRC Committee, *Concluding Observations: Austria* (UN Doc. CRC/C/15/Add.98, 1999),
para. 27.
[488] Seven years before, concerning Canada, the CRC Committee in 1995 only stated that
'[d]eprivation of liberty of children, particularly unaccompanied children, for security or

cations may take several years'. Accordingly, the Committee recommended with reference also to Article 37 to '[r]efrain, as a matter of policy, from detaining unaccompanied minors and ensure the right to speedily challenge the legality of detention, in compliance with article 37 of the Convention. In any case, detention must always be a measure of last resort and for the shortest appropriate period of time'.[489]

135. While in earlier comments to States Parties the Committee usually only made rather general mention[490] of disregard for the principle of last resort, the more recent Committee recommendations address problems with some detail. Libya was disapproved of criminalisation of status offences, requiring vagrant and street children to be placed in juvenile homes, with the ensuing Committee's call to ensure the principles of last resort and shortest period of time.[491] In regard to Madagascar, the Committee was concerned about 'the frequent recourse to and the excessive length of pre-trial detention' and recommended over-all compliance with the principle of last resort, in particular to educational measures, and to 'limit by law the length of pre-trial detention'.[492] Sri Lanka was asked to provide 'adequate alternatives to deprivation of liberty, such as community service orders', in order to overcome the lack in legislation to offer sentencing alternatives, thus leading to young children to be 'sent to prison when a lesser punishment could have been applied'.[493]

136. Turning, more specifically, to the principle of 'shortest appropriate period of time', the Committee was concerned about cases in New Zealand where children 'may even be detained in police cells for several months'.[494] It should be noted here,

---

other purposes should only be used as a measure of last resort in accordance with article 37(b) of the Convention', UN Doc. CRC/C/15/Add.37, 1995, para. 24.

[489] CRC Committee, *Concluding Observations: the United Kingdom* (UN Doc. CRC/C/15/Add.188, 2002), paras. 49, 50(a).

[490] *Cf.* for instance, CRC Committee, *Concluding Observations: Lebanon* (UN Doc. CRC/C/15/Add.54, 1996) para. 44; in respect to Ghana the Committee expressed 'particular concern' about 'the inadequacy of existing alternative measures to imprisonment': CRC Committee, *Concluding Observations: Ghana* (UN Doc. CRC/C/15/Add.73, 1997), para. 27. Lao People's Democratic Republic was encouraged to 'explore alternatives to institutional care as well as traditional mechanisms of conciliation, as long as the principles and guarantees of the Convention are respected': CRC Committee, *Concluding Observations: Lao People's Democratic Republic* (UN Doc. CRC/C/15/Add.78, 1997), para. 53.

[491] CRC Committee, *Concluding Observations: Libyan Arab Jamahiriya* (UN Doc. CRC/C/15/Add.209, 2003), para. 45. As far as status offences are concerned the Committee, at its Day of General Discussion on State violence against children, recommended that 'States parties review all relevant legislation to ensure that children under 18, who are in need of protection are not considered as offenders (including legislation dealing with abandonment, vagrancy, prostitution, migrant status, "truancy", runaways, *etc.*) but are dealt with under child protection mechanisms': UN Doc. CRC/C/97, 2000, para. 688.

[492] CRC Committee, *Concluding Observations: Madagascar* (UN Doc. CRC/C/15/Add.218, 2003), paras 67, 69.

[493] CRC Committee, *Concluding Observations: Sri Lanka* (UN Doc. CRC/C/15/Add.184, 2002), paras. 52, 53.

[494] CRC Committee, *Concluding Observations: New Zealand* (UN Doc. CRC/C/15/Add.216, 2003), para. 49.

that the Human Rights Committee, in its General Comment No. 8 (1982) has considered that, in line with Article 9(3) of the CCPR, any person arrested or detained in a criminal case has to be brought promptly before a judge or other officer authorized by law to exercise judicial power, noting that in its view, 'delays must not exceed a few days'.[495] And with regard to adjudication, Article 10(2)(b) of the CCPR expressly provides that children have to be brought even 'as speedily as possible' before the competent organ.[496]

137. Pre-trial detention 'as long as a year' before the case was dealt with by the court, was not acceptable to the CRC Committee.[497] The Committee was likewise concerned about 'delays in judicial proceedings leading to long periods of pre-trial detention' for children in Greece; and that children can be sentenced to 20 years of imprisonment, calling for abolishment of those provisions.[498] In relation to Japan, the Committee criticized parts of a recent reform of the juvenile justice system as 'not in the spirit of' the CRC principles, in particular the doubling of the limit of pre-trial detention from four to eight weeks.[499]

3. Conditions and Treatment during Deprivation of Liberty

3.1 Treatment with Humanity and Respect for Human Dignity and the Needs of the Child

138. In the discussion on Article 37(b), attention was devoted mainly to circumstances leading to deprivation of liberty; the focus, now, lies with standards set by Article 37(c) during deprivation of liberty. The CRC obliges States to ensure that '[e]very child deprived of liberty shall be treated with humanity and respect for the inherent dignity of the human person, and in a manner which takes into account the needs of persons of his or her age'. The restriction of persons to closed locations naturally creates situations of power imbalances and dependencies, and abuse and exploitation is likely to occur in such settings. The purpose of this fundamen-

---

[495] Human Rights Committee, *General Comment No. 8 (1982): Right to liberty and security of persons, o.c.* (note 308), para. 2.

[496] M. Nowak, *o.c.* (note 255), Article 10, para. 21. An identical clause was initially also contained in the drafting Working Group's proposal after the first reading (UN Doc. E/CN.4/ 1988/WG.1/WP.1/Rev.2, pp. 23–25), but was lost in the ensuing split of provisions into today's Articles 37 and 40. Interestingly also, differing from the English phrase 'shortest appropriate period of time', the similarly authentic text of Art. 37(b) in French uses more urgent wording, speaking of '*une durée aussi brève que possible*'.

[497] CRC Committee, *Concluding Observations: Jamaica* (UN Doc. CRC/C/15/Add.210, 2003), para. 56(c).

[498] CRC Committee, *Concluding Observations: Greece* (UN Doc. CRC/C/15/Add.170, 2002), paras. 78, 79(f).

[499] CRC Committee, *Concluding Observations: Japan* (UN Doc. CRC/C/15/Add.231, 2004), para. 53; on the prohibition of retrogressive measures, *cf. supra* Part II, Chapter III/2.2.3.

tal provision is therefore to uphold the respect for all rights of the person deprived of personal liberty to the greatest extent possible in such circumstances. In the words of the Human Rights Committee, which issued a General Comment on the CRC provision's predecessor, Article 10(1) of the CCPR: 'Persons deprived of their liberty enjoy all the rights set forth in the Covenant, subject to the restrictions that are unavoidable in a closed environment'. Thus, 'respect for the dignity of such persons must be guaranteed under the same conditions as for that of free persons' and 'neither may they be subject to any hardship or constraint other than that resulting from the deprivation of liberty'.[500] The Committee also uses a broad scope of application for these standards, which includes 'any one deprived of liberty under the laws and authority of the State who is held in prisons, hospitals—particularly psychiatric hospitals—detention camps or correctional institutions or elsewhere'.[501]

139. The qualification added by Article 37(c) in respect to the needs of children highlights a specific child development-orientation within the general principle. The reference to the child's age conveys the message that children should not be regarded as one homogenous group, but instead that the conditions and the treatment of the young persons have to be constantly monitored and flexibly adapted due to their personal development.[502] One specific aspect of the general rule for respectful, child development-oriented treatment concerns the separation of children deprived from their liberty from adults, another aspect the right of the child to maintain contacts with the family; both are covered in the second sentence of Article 37(c).

140. As a consequence, Article 37(c) creates a comprehensive set of positive obligations for States Parties to guarantee implementation of this principle in practice. Here, provision of a broad range of services and infrastructure comes into play: the JDL Rules, under section IV (Management of juvenile facilities), requires authorities to establish systems for admission, registration, classification, record-keeping, movement and transfer of children deprived of their liberty, to provide adequate physical environments and accommodation, to offer educational services, vocational training, work and recreational opportunities, enable the child to satisfy his or her religious needs, provide medical facilities, ensure contacts of the child to the outside world, maintain support for preparation to release and establish complaint and monitoring systems; at the same time, the JDL Rules call for qualified personnel to maintain the respective detention facility etc, including 'a sufficient number of specialists such as educators, vocational instructors, counsellors, social workers, psychiatrists and psychologists', 'normally employed on a permanent

---

[500] Human Rights Committee, *General Comment No. 21 (1992): Replaces general comment 9 concerning humane treatment of persons deprived of liberty (Art. 10)*, o.c. (note 308), para. 3.
[501] *Ibid.*, para. 2.
[502] *Cf.* the CRC's concept of evolving capacities of the child, G. Van Bueren, o.c. (note 239), p. 219.

basis'.[503] Of course, such personnel requires specific training as well, *e.g.* on disciplinary procedures and non-violent conflict resolution. It quickly becomes clear from this overview that a considerable level of commitment has to be taken by the government to ensure these standards.

141. The Human Rights Committee has further stressed that this obligation constitutes 'a fundamental and universally applicable rule', which 'cannot be dependent on the material resources available in the State party' and that the principle of non-discrimination must be ensured.[504] Moreover, these standards are relevant irrespective of the lawfulness of the deprivation of liberty.[505] Finally, the Human Rights Committee has declared that Article 10(1) constitutes 'a norm of general international law' which is not subject to derogation under situations of public emergency,[506] which should be accepted for the related provision of Article 37(c) with almost identical content as well.

142. Article 37(c) bears close relationship to the standards prescribed in Article 37(a) of the CRC, as the prohibition of torture or other cruel, inhuman or degrading treatment or punishment may be regarded as one specific qualification of the general rule of treatment with respect and dignity.[507] Rule 67 of the JDL Rules provides for a strict standard on permissible disciplinary measures, banning any cruel, inhuman or degrading treatment, 'including corporal punishment, placement in a dark cell, closed or solitary confinement or any other punishment that may compromise the physical or mental health of the juvenile concerned'. Similarly, in 2000 the CRC Committee recommended to States Parties broadly to 'review all relevant legislation to ensure that all forms of violence against children, however light, are prohibited, including the use of torture, or cruel, inhuman or degrading treatment (such as flogging, corporal punishment or other violent measures), for punishment

---

[503] Rule 81 of the JDL Rules.

[504] Human Rights Committee, *General Comment No. 21 (1992): Replaces general comment 9 concerning humane treatment of persons deprived of liberty (Art. 10)*, *o.c.* (note 308), para. 4. In this context, the Human Rights Committee refers to a wide set of additional non-treaty standards adopted in the field of administration of justice and relevant for the treatment of persons deprived of their liberty, including: the Standard Minimum Rules for the Treatment of Prisoners (1955), the Body of Principles for the Protection of All Persons under Any Form of Detention or Imprisonment (1988), the Code of Conduct for Law Enforcement Officials (1978) and the Principles of Medical Ethics relevant to the Role of Health Personnel, particularly Physicians, in the Protection of Prisoners and Detainees against Torture and Other Cruel, Inhuman or Degrading Treatment or Punishment (1982).

[505] M. Nowak, *o.c.* (note 255), Article 10, para. 8.

[506] Human Rights Committee, *General Comment No. 29 (2001): States of Emergency (article 4)*, *o.c.* (note 308), para. 13(a).

[507] For a closer look at the prohibition of torture under Article 37(a), *Cf. supra* Part I. On a more general level, also Article 3(3) of the CRC should be recalled, requiring comprehensive quality standards and monitoring for all 'institutions, services and facilities for the care or protection of children', including detention centres *etc.*

or disciplining within the child justice system, or in any other context'.[508] In addition, the Committee emphasized both the need for safeguards against impunity of perpetrators violating those standards and for the provision of rehabilitation for victims of such abuses (cf. Article 39). In order to maintain the necessary standards, both effective internal complaint and external monitoring mechanisms are of crucial importance, including international on-site visiting systems as foreseen under the European Convention on the Prevention of Torture and the new CAT Optional Protocol.[509]

143. The CRC Committee has addressed quite frequently poor standards for children deprived of their liberty. In regard to detained asylum-seeking children in the United Kingdom, the Committee raised the issue of access to health and education for these children and recommended to accommodate them rather under a 'children in need' social service regime.[510] It critically assessed States parties practice in relation to independent regular examination,[511] the limited number of teachers working in the juvenile justice system[512] and matters of discipline during deprivation of liberty; here, it called for the prohibition of 'corporal punishment, including whipping and caning, and solitary confinement, in all detention facilities for juvenile offenders, including police stations'[513] and to ensure protection from ill-treatment and extraction of confessions to offences at police stations.[514] The CRC Committee has also started to include recommendations by other human rights treaty bodies, like the CAT Committee, in its own recommendations.[515]

3.2   Separation of Children and Contact with the Family

144. The expression 'in particular' at the beginning of Article 37(c) second sentence links the separation requirement to the overall principle of respectful treatment

---

[508] CRC Committee, *Day of General Discussion: State violence against children (22 September 2000)* (UN Doc. CRC/C/97, 2000), para. 688(8).

[509] With its broad JDL definition of deprivation of liberty as the basis for its Committee's mandate.

[510] CRC Committee, Concluding Observations: *the United Kingdom* (UN Doc. CRC/C/15/Add.188, 2002), para. 50.

[511] CRC Committee, Concluding Observations: *Madagascar* (UN Doc. CRC/C/15/Add.218, 2003), para. 69.

[512] CRC Committee, Concluding Observations: *Burkina Faso* (UN Doc. CRC/C/15/Add.193, 2002), para. 60.

[513] CRC Committee, Concluding Observations: *Singapore* (UN Doc. CRC/C/15/Add.220, 2003), para. 45. Cf. also B. Abramson, o.c. (note 247), I/2, in relation to the need for outright condemnation of the practice of flogging in closed institutions.

[514] CRC Committee, Concluding Observations: *St. Vincent and the Grenadines* (UN Doc. CRC/C/15/Add.184, 2002), paras. 52 and 53.

[515] CRC Committee, Concluding Observations: *Kazakhstan* (UN Doc. CRC/C/15/Add.213, 2003), para. 36 (under the heading of civil rights and freedoms): 'The Committee concurs with the content of the recommendations adopted by the Committee against Torture which are relevant to the situation of children below the age of 18'.

in the first sentence and establishes more specific positive State obligations. It is remarkable here to note that on the one hand, the principle of keeping children separate from adults ranks among the oldest of UN standards in the field of criminal justice,[516] aiming at prevention of a negative impact on the child in adult setting, but on the other hand, its compliance still meets persistent difficulties in States Parties practice. One indicator for this assessment might be found already in the relatively high number of reservations under international law to this guarantee; in fact, almost all reservations relating to Article 37(b), (c), (d) standards concern the separation of children from adults. Some States openly state that they do not deem such separation 'appropriate',[517] others frankly admit lack of adequate facilities.[518] While the latter raises questions of the government's commitment to ensure CRC standards, the first argument seems particularly odd, as the CRC already does allow for some flexibility in this regard.[519] Still, the explicit reference to the best interests of the child clause in Article 37(c) second sentence qualifies this flexibility as a child-focussed exception only, excluding exceptions *e.g.* for budgetary considerations of the government. Moreover, this clause demands for respect of the child's right to participation in that decision in line with Article 12(1), but also taking into account the need for information according to Article 9(4) of the CRC.[520]

145. In relation to Article 10(2) of the CCPR, the Human Rights Committee does not consider necessary the construction of separate buildings for adults and children, but to establish at least separate quarters for those groups.[521] Similarly, Rule 13(4) of the Beijing Rules provides for children to be 'detained in a separate institution or in a separate part of an institution also holding adults'. The 1955 Standard Minimum Rules for the Treatment of Prisoners contain further categories of persons deprived of their liberty to stay separated, including men/women and

---

[516] Rule 8 of the 1957 UN Standard Minimum Rules for the Treatment of Prisoners; for critical remarks on the failure of CRC States Parties towards ensuring the separation principle and a critical assessment of the CRC Committee practice in this regard, *cf.* B. Abramson, *o.c.* (note 247), I/2.

[517] *Cf.* Canada: 'The Government of Canada accepts the general principles of article 37(c) of the Convention, but reserves the right not to detain children separately from adults where this is not appropriate or feasible'.

[518] Or a combination of both arguments, *cf.*: 'The Government of New Zealand reserves the right not to apply article 37(c) in circumstances where the shortage of suitable facilities makes the mixing of juveniles and adults unavoidable; and further reserves the right not to apply article 37(c) where the interests of other juveniles in an establishment require the removal of a particular juvenile offender or where mixing is considered to be of benefit to the persons concerned'.

[519] The corresponding provision in Article 10(2)(b) of the CCPR had been criticised by states for its absolute character prohibiting exceptions; this was explicitly taken into account during the CRC drafting; *cf.* also G. Van Bueren, *o.c.* (note 239), p. 219.

[520] *Ibid.*, p. 220; *cf*, moreover, on the unresolved issue of (small) children in detention in order to stay with members of their family, at pp. 226 and 227.

[521] M. Nowak, *o.c.* (note 255), Article 10, para. 19.

untried/convicted prisoners (Rule 8). The latter group is also included in Article 10(2)(a) of the CCPR and standards apply to both adults and children.[522]

146. The CRC Committee has frequently reminded governments of their obligation to keep children separated, in order to ensure their protection from negative impact of adult offenders. Towards Tunisia, concern was voiced over 'detention of juveniles with adults which has resulted in sexual abuse or other ill-treatment', recommending treatment of children in conflict with the law 'in a different and distinct manner so that they are not placed in the same institutions with the same regime or restrictions'.[523] The joint detention of children with persons up to 25 years in Germany was also disapproved by the Committee.[524] In regard to Kyrgyzstan, the Committee criticized that 'juveniles, in particular girls, are being detained with adults'.[525]

147. Article 37(c) second sentence, finally, contains the child's right to maintain contacts with the family during deprivation of liberty, through visits or correspondence. And again, an exception clause was inserted, for instance, in cases where continued contact of the child with the parents might have a negative impact on his or her situation. In any case, as Van Bueren notes, 'it is clear that it is an exception, which should be exercised only in accordance with the child's best interests and not imposed as a disciplinary measure or as a means of securing the child's cooperation'.[526] And recourse to that exception has, again, to take into account the views of the child, in accordance with Article 12 of the CRC.

148. The Committee occasionally raised the issue of contact with the family in its discussion with the States Parties, expressing rather general concern about the lack of access[527] or recommending the government to ensure 'regular contact' with their families.[528] 'The absence of a formal obligation to inform parents about the detention' of the child caused concern to the Committee, recommending introduction of such a provision.[529]

---

[522] *Cf.* also Rule 17 and 18 of the JDL Rule, stressing also the need to treat untried children in accordance with the presumption of innocence, *e.g.* to work voluntarily only. The CRC Committee has also already taken up this issue, *cf.*, for example, *Concluding Observations: Jordan* (UN Doc. CRC/C/15/Add.21, 1994), para. 16.

[523] CRC Committee, *Concluding Observations: Tunisia* (UN Doc. CRC/C/15/Add.181, 2002), paras. 45, 46(c).

[524] CRC Committee, *Concluding Observations: Germany* (UN Doc. CRC/C/15/Add.226, 2004), para. 60.

[525] CRC Committee, Concluding Observations: *Kyrgyzstan* (UN Doc. CRC/C/15/Add.244, 2004), para. 66.

[526] *Ibid.*, p. 220, with further discussion also on the relationship to Article 9(4) of the CRC.

[527] *Concluding Observations: Russian Federation* (UN Doc. CRC/C/15/Add.4, 1993), para. 14; *Nigeria* (UN Doc. CRC/C/15/Add.61, 1996), para. 23.

[528] CRC Committee, *Concluding Observations: Morocco* (UN Doc. CRC/C/15/Add.211), para. 68; and *Pakistan* (UN Doc. CRC/C/15/Add.217, 2003), para. 81.

[529] CRC Committee, *Concluding Observations: Burkina Faso* (UN Doc. CRC/C/15/Add.193, 2002), paras. 60 and 62.

3.3   *Review of Deprivation of Liberty—Assistance and Prompt Decision*

149. Article 37(d) of the CRC contains important procedural guarantees for children deprived of their liberty: the right to prompt access to legal and other assistance, the right to challenge the legality of the decision leading to deprivation of liberty and the right to a prompt decision on this matter.

150. Any decision on deprivation of liberty must be subject to a review process—this represents a crucial safeguarding element derived from the principle of *habeas corpus*, already indicating its long-standing origins. It is concerned specifically with the legality[530] of the deprivation of liberty itself, independently of the right to appeal in criminal matters (*e.g.* Article 2 ECHR Protocol No. 7). Article 37(d) provides this right to all situations of deprivation of liberty; this bears relevance particularly in those cases outside the regular criminal justice field, *i.e.* cases of administrative detention or custodial orders under a child welfare system. The reference to a 'court or other competent, independent and impartial authority' indicates that the decision needs not be taken necessarily by a ordinary court, but any organ meeting the requirements listed;[531] in particular, emphasis on the organ's competence has to be placed, meaning that the respective authority must have both the power to review the legality of the deprivation of liberty and the power to order the immediate release if found to be unlawful.[532]

151. The decision on the legality has to be taken 'promptly', which points to the objective that compared to the corresponding Article 9(4) of the CCPR ('without delay'), a more speedy approach is warranted in the case of deprivation of liberty of a child.[533] As an indication, the Human Rights Committee practice, under the CCPR, refers in that context to periods of several weeks, but less than three months.[534] The CRC Committee, in examining the situation in Bolivia, has expressed concern that 'a child may remain in custody for the excessively long period of 45 days before the legality of his or her detention is decided upon'.[535]

152. Not least for a meaningful preparation of the review process, the CRC accords every child the subjective right to prompt access to legal and other appropriate assistance. The CRC Committee, which asks for any time-limit thereto in its Guidelines

---

[530]   Again, in regard to domestic as well as international standards, *cf. supra* Part II, Chapter III/2.5.

[531]   *Cf.* Article 14(1) of the CCPR, and the Human Rights Committee, *General Comment No. 13 (1984): Equality before the courts and the right to a fair and public hearing by an independent court established by law (Art. 14)*, *o.c.* (note 308), para. 4.

[532]   *Cf.* M. Nowak, *o.c.* (note 255), Article 9, para. 51, on the comparable provision of Article 9(4) of the CCPR.

[533]   The Commentary on Rule 20 of the Beijing Rules states that the 'speedy conduct of formal procedures in juvenile cases is a paramount concern'.

[534]   *Cf.* M. Nowak, *o.c.* (note 255), Article 9, para. 51 with further references.

[535]   CRC Committee, *Concluding Observations: Bolivia* (UN Doc. CRC/C/15/Add.1, 1993), para. 11.

for Periodic Reports, stresses the character of the individual child's right and crit-icized, again in relation to Bolivia, that 'the age for legal counselling without parental consent is unclear and practices in this regard may not be in conformity with arti-cle 37(d)'.[536] Access to a lawyer has to be guaranteed to the child in pre-trial deten-tion[537] and Switzerland was asked to 'systematize' legal assistance to children in pre-trial detention;[538] furthermore, legal assistance should be free to children.[539] In a related area, with reference to the right to appeal, the Committee recommended to Burkina Faso to amend legislation 'to allow children to appeal a decision with-out their parents'.[540] Moreover, the Committee regularly stresses the need for effec-tive complaint procedures in general, and calls for the establishment of an 'independent, child-sensitive and accessible complaint system for children' within the administration of juvenile justice context.[541] In regard to Italy, the Committee specifically recommended to '[a]llow periodic visits to the Reception Centres and Penal Institutes for Minors by impartial and independent bodies', and lastly, asked for 'training on children's rights to those responsible for administering juvenile justice'.[542]

Bibliography

Bradley, C. A., 'The Juvenile Death Penalty and International Law', *Duke Law Journal* 52, 2002, p. 486;

Hamilton, C. and Harvey, R., 'The Role of the Public Opinion in the Implementation of International Juvenile Justice Standards', *International Journal of Children's Rights* 11, 2004, pp. 369–390;

International Crime Centre for Criminal Law Reform and Criminal Justice Policy/UN African Institute for the Prevention of Crime and the Treatment of Offenders/Uganda Prisons Service, *Alternatives to Incarceration: their Applicability and Practice in Uganda*, Kampala, 1998;

---

[536] *Ibid.*, para. 11.

[537] CRC Committee, *Concluding Observations: Romania* (UN Doc. CRC/C/15/Add.199, 2003), para. 63.

[538] CRC Committee, *Concluding Observations: Switzerland* (UN Doc. CRC/C/15/Add.182, 2002), para. 58. With regard to the United Kingdom, a review of the 'availability and effectiveness of legal representation and other forms of independent advocacy' for refugee children was asked for by the Committee, UN Doc. CRC/C/15/Add.188, 2002, para. 50.

[539] CRC Committee, *Concluding Observations: St. Vincent and the Grenadines* (UN Doc. CRC/C/15/Add.184, 2002), para. 53.

[540] CRC Committee, *Concluding Observations: Burkina Faso* (UN Doc. CRC/C/15/Add.193, 2002), para. 62(e).

[541] CRC Committee, *Concluding Observations: Burkina Faso* (UN Doc. CRC/C/15/Add.193, 2002); para. 62(j) and Italy (UN Doc. CRC/C/15/Add.198, 2003, paras. 51 and 53. Additionally, it also asked for investigation and prosecution of any case of mistreatment by law enforcement personnel, Madagascar, UN Doc. CRC/C/15/Add.218, 2003, para. 69. *Cf.* R. Hodgkin and Peter Newell, *o.c.* (note 319), p. 555; *cf.* also the conceptually related right to review in Article 25.

[542] CRC Committee, *Concluding Observations: Italy* (UN Doc. CRC/C/15/Add.198, 2003), para. 53.

Nanda, Ved. P., 'The United States Reservation to the Ban on the Death Penalty for Juvenile Offenders: An Appraisal Under the International Covenant on Civil and Political Rights', *DePaul Law Review* 42, 1993, p. 1311;

Schabas, W. A., *The Abolition of the Death Penalty in International Law* (3rd ed. Cambridge, Cambridge University Press), 2003;

Schabas, W. A., 'The Death Penalty for Crimes Committed by Persons Under Eighteen Years of Age', in: E. Verhellen (ed.), *Monitoring Children's Rights* (Dordrecht: Martinus Nijhoff, 1996), pp. 603–619;

Sparks R., Girling E. and Smith M., 'Children talking about justice and punishment', *International Journal of Children's Rights* 8, 2000, pp. 191–209;

van Zyl Smit, D. 'Abolishing Life Imprisonment', *Punishment and Society* 3, 2001, p. 299;

Weissbrodt, D. 'Execution of Juvenile Offenders by the United States Violates International Human Rights Law', *American University Journal of International Law and Policy* 3, 1988, p. 339;

UN Office of the High Commissioner for Human Rights/International Bar Association, *Human Rights in the Administration of Justice: A Manual on Human Rights for Judges, Prosecutors and Lawyers*, Professional Training Series No. 9 (New York—Geneva, UN Publication, 2003).